The United States Of Europe And Other Papers

THE UNITED STATES OF EUROPE

SIR ARTHUR SALTER

THE UNITED STATES OF
EUROPE

AND OTHER PAPERS

By the Author of
RECOVERY

Edited with Notes by

W. Arnold-Forster

REYNAL AND HITCHCOCK INC.
NEW YORK

PREFACE

IT has been my habit, for many years of my life as an official, to commit to writing my reflections on the wider aspects of the questions presenting themselves for current decision and action. My object was a double one: first, to clear my own mind and make it easier to decide upon such detailed steps as were within my own competence by some conception of wider policy; and secondly, when I had opinions on questions extending beyond my own activities, to influence my colleagues, or others whose views were likely to determine policy.

Such papers are not official documents. They are rather in the nature of a record in writing of the kind of arguments in discussion in which any official interested in his work is constantly engaged with others of like interests.

It has been suggested to me that some of the papers which I have written under these conditions during my ten years of work with the League of Nations are of sufficient interest to justify publication. They have of course none of the authority of official documents. They merely represent the impact upon a single mind of the passing events and tendencies of opinion which constituted the environment in which the League and its policy developed during its first formative years. But they may cover some ground for which published official documents are lacking; and they perhaps throw some light upon the way in which discussion by officials contributes, amid other influences, to the formation of policy.

Some of the papers originally written for the above purposes were later converted into official documents, and as such (except for one or two which have already been published officially) they have been excluded from the present collection; and the notes now printed are of course only a selection from a much greater number.

In a few instances a sentence or passage including a personal criticism has been omitted; and here and there a verbal crudity has been corrected. Otherwise the papers remain as originally written; there has been no change whatever of substance or omission of any opinion subsequently shown to be erroneous.

In some cases of course later experience has disproved anticipations; and changed the views of the writer; or a policy different from that advocated has been pursued. In other cases policy has proceeded along the lines recommended. As regards these latter cases I am anxious to avoid any suggestion that a *post hoc* is a *propter hoc*. The papers as written usually reflected strong trends of current opinion, entertained by many persons interested and influential in League policy; the papers themselves may sometimes have been a contributory, they were rarely a determining, factor in the formation of policy.

I am greatly indebted to my friend, Mr. W. Arnold-Forster, for the laborious work he has undertaken of editing and annotating these papers and presenting both the setting in which they were written and the sequence of later events.

A. S.

CONTENTS

CHAPTER   PAGE

       PREFACE   7

PART I

THE UNITED STATES OF EUROPE

I. THE ORGANIZATION OF THE LEAGUE OF NATIONS [1919]   13

II. A PROPOSAL FOR A WORLD ECONOMIC CONFERENCE [1925]   32

III. THE LEAGUE AND AMERICA   45

IV. THE ALTERNATIVE TO A REGIONAL LEAGUE [1926]   53

V. THREE COUNCILS OR FOUR? [1927]   71

VI. THE "UNITED STATES OF EUROPE" IDEA [1929]   83

VII. THE FRENCH MEMORANDUM ON A EUROPEAN FEDERAL UNION [1930]   105

VIII. THE INTERNATIONAL CHARACTER OF THE LEAGUE SECRETARIAT [1930]   125

PART II

THE WEAPONS OF THE LEAGUE

IX. THE ECONOMIC WEAPONS OF THE LEAGUE UNDER ARTICLE XVI OF THE COVENANT [1919]   142

X. ECONOMIC SANCTIONS AND THE GENEVA PROTOCOL [1924]   160

CHAPTER   PAGE

XI. THE GRECO-BULGAR INCIDENT [1925]   170

XII. IF THE UNITED STATES JOINED THE LEAGUE
     [1926]   189

XIII. ARBITRATION, SECURITY, AND DISARMAMENT:
      FOUR NOTES [1927]   204

XIV. THE KELLOGG PACT.   I. MARCH, 1928   230

                         II. AUGUST, 1928   235

XV. FOOD SHIPS. PRESIDENT HOOVER'S PROPOSAL
    FOR IMMUNITY [1929]   252

XVI. FREEDOM OF THE SEAS [1929]   262

XVII. NOTES ON SECURITY AND CONFIDENCE [1931]   271

     APPENDIX.   THE COVENANT OF THE LEAGUE
     OF NATIONS   279

     INDEX   297

PART I

THE UNITED STATES OF EUROPE

CHAPTER I

THE ORGANIZATION OF THE LEAGUE OF NATIONS

Author's Note

THE main interest of this paper depends upon its very early date—before the Treaty of Versailles was signed or even its text fixed in its final form.

I have made it a rule to refrain, myself, from any comments, in the light of later experience, upon the opinions expressed in the following papers. As the sole exception to this rule, I think it well to note that the opinion expressed in this early paper (on page 25), as to the appointment of Geneva National Secretaries, was immediately changed. It is an instance of a principle being momentarily abandoned under the influence of a special environment. Writing during the Peace Conference at Paris, where there was an unprecedented concentration of the principal political personalities of the world, I was strongly impressed by the danger that the League, with its headquarters not in a great political capital but in the University city of Geneva, would be isolated from the sources of political strength without which its great tasks would be impossible; and for the moment felt that other considerations must be subordinated to diminishing this danger.

The real safeguard against the danger of the League drifting into a political backwater, however, is the one for which it is so greatly indebted to Sir Austen Chamberlain, i.e. the habit of regular attendance at the Council by the Foreign Ministers of the principal European countries. This makes the presence of resident national Secretaries or Delegates of such countries at Geneva unnecessary, and undesirable. The situation is of course quite different in the case of more distant countries.

A. S.

THE ORGANIZATION OF THE LEAGUE OF NATIONS

MAY 10, 1919

GENERAL CONCEPTION OF THE LEAGUE

The nature of the League's organization must necessarily depend upon the conception which those arranging it have of the scope of its work, and of the extent to which it will affect the current work of the national Governments of the world. At the one extreme the League may only touch political questions at the point at which they are visibly causing or about to cause serious international disputes, and its remaining work will be mainly that of handling or co-ordinating a mass of non-contentious business (postal conventions, supervision of waterways, etc.). On this conception the Governments of the world would in international as well as domestic affairs remain essentially national and separatist. Each Government's policy would be developed through a complete departmental organization formed and decided upon by the national Cabinet, and communicated, when communication was necessary, to other Governments through one medium—the Foreign Office.

At the other extreme the League may be conceived of as ultimately becoming an integral factor in the determination of the policy of every national Government in the world so far as policy affects other countries, both the government and the administration of the world in international affairs becoming gradually, but really and effectively, international. On this conception the policy of the several nations in international matters would not be merely adjusted by the negotiation of separate national decisions, but, to a large extent, actually formed and developed by international consultation both between departmental Ministers and departmental officials.

Some of the implications of this conception will appear from the later section of this note which describes the leading principles of international economic administration during the latter part of the war.

On the least ambitious forecast the League will doubtless go beyond the first conception, and on the most ambitious it will certainly for many years fall far short of the second, but the organization must from the first be based largely on one or other conception of its main character and ultimate tendency.

It is on the assumption that the second and more ambitious conception is accepted as the true one that the following notes are written.

ADVERSE FACTORS

On this assumption it is necessary first to point out the very strong forces which will tend to limit the work of the League to the less ambitious rôle. The inevitable tendency of the war has been to develop and increase national and separatist feeling. During hostilities this separatism was controlled and concealed by the overriding necessity of common action. Now that hostilities have ceased the unifying force has disappeared, and the immense strength of separate national feeling and divergent national interest is at once apparent. Instead of the visible necessities of a war in progress, we have only the fear of a possible future war as the foundation of the League of Nations. The consequence is that the League starts towards internationalism from a nationalism that is in some respects more developed and more intense than before the war commenced.

In the second place the location of the League, however necessary, at Geneva—which is outside and remote from the main political and economic currents of the world, which is not a very accessible place of conference for responsible and overburdened Ministers, and has no very inspiring associations or traditions— will be an immense handicap.

In the third place the mass of useful and non-contentious, but dull and unambitious, work which will perhaps form the greater part of the actual earlier work of the League's organization may well have the effect of making the League, in the eyes of the world and indeed of its own members and officials, an international instrument which is improved and more effective indeed, but not essentially different from The Hague.

It must also be remembered that the instinctive attitude of every national Government and every national Department towards an international organization in another country which attempts to affect national policy is, always and necessarily to begin with, a mixture of ignorance, indifference, and irritation.

The constitution of the League so far as prescribed in the Covenant is certainly not in itself sufficient to counteract these forces. An Assembly which meets once in two years; an Executive Council which is not required to meet more than once a year,[1] and which, though doubtless intended to meet more frequently, will not apparently be in constant session; and an official organization consisting of persons who will presumably be required by the acceptance of office to divest themselves of any specifically national point of view, and in doing so to cut themselves off necessarily from any constant contact with and responsibility to the several national Governments, would in themselves prove entirely inadequate.

THE DANGER OF PROVINCIALISM

After the first few months of comparative enthusiasm, during which the Executive Council will be in session and considerable publicity will be given to its work, the danger is that we may see the League represented by a denationalized official staff, living in a provincial capital, cut off from any live contact with any of the real instruments of government throughout the world, inadequately supplied even with information as to the proposals and contemplated policies of the several national Governments in all the questions that really matter, handling and co-ordinating a great mass of

[1] This was written before it was known how the Covenant would be operated. In practice the Assembly meets once a year, and the Council three times (in addition to special Sessions). Meetings of this frequency are, however, not prescribed by the Covenant.—A. S., Feb. 1933.

dull and useful work which is given to them because it is non-contentious in character, and is for that reason quite irrelevant to the future peace of the world, and then, at the point when a dispute has actually broken out, intervening at the last hour as a somewhat improved Hague Tribunal. Such a League of Nations may well serve a useful purpose in co-ordinating and developing non-contentious international departmental work, and may also serve to prevent the wars, both of smaller nations, and such of the wars of larger nations as result from mere inadequacy of negotiation, and from the military necessity which a country expecting to fight has in getting in the first blow. But it is quite clear that if this is the line of organization, it will have little effect upon the development of the more fundamental causes of international conflict. It will be no vital and integral part of the government of the world.

The great danger of the League, in a word, is that it will die of dullness. Geneva will be a suburb, not a centre, in the world's government.

INTERNATIONAL ADMINISTRATION IN ECONOMIC SPHERE
DURING WAR

Before proceeding to make certain suggestions with a view to meeting this danger, it may be convenient to state a few of the leading principles of international administration as it had developed in the economic sphere by the end of the war. It is of course fully recognized that both the character of the work and the compelling necessity of co-operative action arising from the war created conditions very different from those in which the League necessarily starts. These conditions, within a large but limited sphere, and for a temporary period, resulted in a developed stage of international administration which may indeed be reached after many years if the general world movement is in that direction, but is much in advance of anything with which a Peace organization can begin. For that very reason, however, the administration as then developed may be useful as illustrating the lines upon which administration so far as it becomes really international tends to develop.

Administration through International Councils.—In the first place throughout the entire economic sphere there was direct contact between the departmental organizations of the Allies. At the commencement of the war communication, e.g. between the Shipping Office of Great Britain and the Shipping Office of France was via the Foreign Office; and when the mass of detailed business got beyond the possibilities of such a method of communication and the *Commission Internationale de Ravitaillement* was established, the same principle was followed, i.e. the Allied representatives in London of whatever Allied Department was dealing with whatever subject were grouped together in one organization and communicated with the several British Departments, not direct, but through a British Officer who exercised in this respect a Foreign Office function. Later in the war, however, the *Commission Internationale de Ravitaillement* and the whole principle on which it was founded were replaced by an organization essentially international in character. This organization, as developed by the Allied Maritime

Transport Council at the end of the war, included machinery under which the Ministers of Munitions of the several Allied countries met directly on the Munitions Council, Food Ministers on a Food Council, and (in fact though not in form above both, since shipping was the limiting factor) Shipping Ministers on the Allied Maritime Transport Council. Not only that, but, throughout the whole range of supplies, the officials of the several Allied Departments met in daily work upon some sixteen Programme Committees and on the Transport Executive of the Transport Council. Throughout this immense sphere, therefore, current work was carried on by direct communication of expert with expert, and not by means of the formulation of a general national policy subsequently communicated from one country to another. The general assumption on which this organization was based was one that was clearly true in the later stages of the war, viz. that, so far as there was any conflict of interest, it was mainly conflict between different services rather than between different countries, e.g. the competition of the Munitions Programme as a whole, both British, French, and Italian, as against the Food Programme as a whole, for a limited amount of total tonnage, was more important than any conflict of interest between the British Munitions Programme and the French Munitions Programme, etc.

Officials in International Administration.—The pivot of the whole scheme was the association of the officials of the different countries in daily administrative work and the relation in which they stood both to their Allied colleagues on the one hand and to their own

Governments through their respective Ministers on the other. It was essential to the proper working of such a scheme that a national representative should be sufficiently in the confidence of his own Government to be able within certain limits to influence its policy, and in sufficiently close and constant touch with the relevant Minister of that Government to know those limits. It was equally essential that he should be working with Allied colleagues whom he trusted and who trusted him. So far as these conditions obtained, it was customary, when some new question of policy, on which Allied co-operation was necessary, required decision, that the question should be discussed frankly, and in its earliest stages, between the several Allied colleagues and before the several Governments had given definite decisions and formulated any national policy. The several national representatives in this way, by stating the considerations likely to move their own Governments and ascertaining similarly those likely to move the other Governments, would attempt between them to arrive at a policy to which the assent of all the Governments concerned could in fact be obtained. The great advantage of this method was that when the Allied Ministers met in conference they had before them (if the work had been done properly) a policy already formulated in such a way as to secure acceptance, instead of having before them several fully formed and rigid national decisions (each with the authority of a Cabinet decision, and, behind it, settled departmental arrangements), and consequently a problem for which an adequate solution was extremely difficult to find. This

process was exemplified at its best by the working of
the Transport Executive in relation to the Transport
Council. Throughout the eight most difficult months
of the war this organization in fact governed and
controlled practically the whole of the Allied supply
system, and arranged immense reductions in the
several service programmes to correspond with the
inadequate tonnage available; but during the whole
of this time the Allied Ministers themselves only found
it necessary to meet four times, and on every one of
these occasions all the recommendations of the Executive and no others were in fact adopted. This did not
mean that the several Ministers had allowed the
officials in fact to determine major policy themselves.
It meant that the Allied officials had throughout their
work been sufficiently informed of the general policy
of their Ministers to know what common policy on
a particular issue could be got through, and the
meetings of the Ministers in fact served as a demonstration that this work had been properly done. It
has not of course been possible to extend the same
method of working to the Supreme Economic Council,
formed since the Armistice; and the contrast between
the working of that Council and the Allied Maritime
Transport Council is very great.

INTERNATIONAL GOVERNMENT

It may be worth while, before proceeding to any
immediate and practical proposals, to attempt to see
what part the League would play in the government
of the world, if the general tendency is towards internationalism, after what would doubtless be a long

period of gradual growth. One may imagine that after such a period of progress no Cabinet Minister in any important Cabinet would propose any policy having important consequences to other countries without an effective prior consideration of those consequences with the corresponding Ministers of other countries. More than that, the policy would under the above principles have been discussed without binding effect between the several national officials working in constant contact in their different spheres before the final national policy had been formed; i.e. it would be subject to real international consultation while still in the actual process of formation. This process one may imagine as applying not only, as it doubtless will, to non-contentious business, such as postal conventions, or even relatively non-contentious work, such as labour legislation, but in time even to the extremely contentious work of devising economic policy.

ECONOMIC WORK OF LEAGUE

I believe the ultimate causes of war are mainly economic; that the fundamentally wrong thing in government is to use the instrument of government to give a commercial advantage either to a section of a community or to one community in competition with others; that the problem of administrative readjustments of the world's government can only become manageable by the League of Nations if administrative responsibility implies no economic advantages; and that the principle adopted in the Covenant for mandatory colonies must, if peace is to be permanently assured, be ultimately extended over the world; and I, therefore, believe that in the end the economic division of a League should be the most important part of its organization. It is obvious, however, that the greatest dangers lie here, and progress must be most gradual. The economic action and the corresponding organization must, therefore, to start with, be modest in character. It is well, however, to have in mind, in first planning it, that it may ultimately have the biggest task to perform; and it is partly for this reason that I suggest that there should be from the start a machinery under which the economic Ministers of the different countries will frequently come into direct contract with each other on International Councils.

PUBLIC OPINION

Whether the League fails or succeeds really depends, however, on the movement of public opinion. This was strongly in favour towards the end of hostilities, and reached its highest point in the acceptance of the principles of President Wilson's policy as expressed in the series of notes ending with the Fourteen Points. Since then there has been a very serious reaction. The elections, the tendency of the Press in the United Kingdom, America, and elsewhere, and the conduct and spirit of the peace negotiations, serve to show clearly that if the real and final opinion of the public is adequately expressed in the present Parliaments, Governments, and Press of the world, the League is hopeless. Nothing can secure it except a strong and new impulse from public opinion outside; but fortunately there are many reasons to believe that there is a strong potential public opinion which may develop the requisite force and impetus.

One of the main tasks of those who handle the League will clearly be so to manage things as to give every chance for this public opinion to develop, and to time their action at different stages with a very close regard to the actual and potential public sentiment of the period.

This consideration has an important bearing on the choice of the Home National Secretaries suggested below.

SUGGESTIONS

With this preface the following general suggestions may be offered.

Geneva National Secretaries.—It seems essential that there should be at the Headquarters of the League, in addition to and separate from the purely non-national staff of the Secretary-General, National Departments of the League under British, French, Italian, and American Secretaries, etc. These Secretaries would be responsible not to the Secretary-General, but to their own Governments. To their own Governments they would represent the international point of view, and to the League they would represent a national point of view. They should in my opinion be paid by and regard themselves as having a primary responsibility to their several national Governments. It would be essential that they should enjoy the complete confidence of their own Governments, and that nothing of the national policy of their own Governments should be concealed from them. They should, for instance, have access to Cabinet Minutes.

Home National Secretaries.—In addition to the Geneva National Secretaries there should be a Home National Secretary of first-rate ability with a strong though small office in the capital of his own country. Probably the Geneva National Secretary in Geneva and the Home National Secretary in London or Paris should be constantly changing places. It would be the constant duty of the Secretaries in London, Paris, etc., to see that the League's point of view was effectively brought to bear upon the policy of every Department, and (doubtless through the National Minister on the Executive Council of the League) on the policy of the country as decided by the Cabinet. It would also be his duty to see that full information was acquired and transmitted to the Secretary in Geneva.

Publicity.—In addition, however, and perhaps most important of all, the National Secretary in London, Paris, Washington, etc., would be responsible for seeing that every possible official encouragement was given to every organization and every movement in his own country in the direction helpful to the League. In each country there will doubtless be, and certainly must be if the League is to be successful, a purely private League of Nations Society or organization supported by private funds. It is essential that these organizations should be as free and spontaneous as possible. At the same time an able National Secretary could do much to inspire, guide, and assist. At this point one comes to perhaps the most difficult and most important problem, and that is the relation of the League and its organization to the Press. If the League is to be successful, it is obvious that there must be immense assistance from the Press in every main country. For this purpose it is equally obvious that no subsidy from League funds can possibly be available. A similar disability does not, however, attach to the use of funds collected by private organizations, though the dangers are obvious. In general it may be said that the most important qualification of the Home National Secretary must be his power to maintain a close personal association with, and exercise a strong personal influence upon, the members of his own Government and the leading persons affecting public opinion throughout the country.

International Councils and International Administration.—If the League is to become gradually an important part of the government of the world, it will not be sufficient to rely on the meeting of the Assembly and the Executive Council. It will be necessary to have a very elastic machinery for effecting *direct contact between the main national Governments of the world under the general auspices of the League.* The relevant Ministers of the several Cabinets will have to be encouraged to meet frequently on bodies such as the Transport Council, Supreme Economic Council, etc., and discuss their national policies so far as they are international in their effect in direct contact with each other. This should apply probably not only to associations of Chancellors of Exchequers and Presidents of the Boards of Trade, on bodies like an Economic Council, but also to similar associations of the Labour Ministers of the

four countries whether or not as part of the Economic
Council, and also to similar associations of the War
Ministers in the different countries; and beyond these
arrangements for occasional meetings of the Allied
Ministers, there should be some form of permanent
association and co-operation of officials who would,
as in the case of the Transport Executive, endeavour
so to adjust the development of national policy within
their respective spheres as to facilitate agreement on
policy when the Ministers actually met.

Association of America.—The problem of America is
one of peculiar difficulty and importance. It is obviously essential, if the League is to be successful, that
America should be in full and complete association.
At the same time the strongest tradition of American
politics is of course to keep clear of Europe, and the
tendency to swing back to this policy now hostilities
are over is at the present moment very marked indeed.
Partly as a consequence of this, and of the great
distance which separates America from Europe, it is
of course particularly difficult for America to delegate
authority to her foreign representatives. Moreover,
when an American representative first arrives, it is
natural that his point of view should often be so
remote from that of Europe as to make agreement
on a common policy very difficult. When, on the
other hand, he has been in Europe long enough to
adjust his point of view to that of European countries,
he will often have lost touch with his own Government
and much of his influence on it. In shipping affairs
in the war, it was found desirable in order to meet
these difficulties to arrange a constant interchange

of American representatives. If America is to be fully associated, there should probably never be a time at which there are no Americans on the Atlantic on their way to or from Geneva.

Location of Permanent Organization.—While the central staff of the League is at Geneva, and while that city will doubtless be used for the greater number of conferences, particularly for such business as adjustment of maritime laws, arrangement of postal conventions, development of international health arrangements, etc., it is of very great importance that there should be frequent meetings of important ministerial bodies for the work of the League in all the main capitals of the world, and probably it would be desirable to divide out several of the main categories of the League's work and arrange for the permanent administrative work to be done in each case in a specified main capital, and for the international Councils dealing with that subject to meet in that capital.

Generally it is suggested that the organization of the League should be both in reality and visibly before the world located, not in Geneva, but in all sections in all the main capitals of the world, Geneva being a co-ordinating secretariat for the whole organization, but not more.

Consultative Trade Organizations.—There should be a machinery similar to that devised during the war (cf. Oilseeds Executive with connected Advisory Committees on Oils and Fats) for enabling effective consultation to take place between international representative Powers, both on the employers' and labour side in all the main industries. This would be a cross division in the general scheme of organization as questions of labour conditions, tariffs, trusts, etc., would be dealt with together as affecting one particular industry or group of industries. Such an organization would doubtless be linked through its official personnel to the meetings of Economic Ministers of the several nations.

Intelligence and Research.—An Intelligence and Research Division, particularly for economic enquiry in the widest sense (including labour conditions as well as general economic statistics), should be a most important part of the organization. The great importance of this rests in the fact that it is possible through such a Division to make substantial progress, and prepare the way for action, on matters which the several countries would never allow to be handled as administrative problems. The sort of problem which might (if internationalism develops) be considered with a view to action ten years hence can at once be advanced by reference to a Research Division. With this in view it is important that the Head of the Division should have an experience and outlook much wider than that of a statistician or actuary.

Greater and Smaller Powers.—Arrangements will doubtless be made throughout the organization to secure that (as in the war organizations and the Peace Conference) there is a kind of inner circle of the great countries (which will in time doubtless include Germany as well as the present main Allies) and an outer circle of the smaller countries. Within the British Empire a special problem arises for which a solution may be found in the analogy of the arrangements

made at the Peace Conference and the Supreme
Economic Council.

If the general conception is at all on the above lines,
it is very undesirable that the detailed organization
should be hurried or prejudiced by premature appointments of personnel or exact specification of functions.
Probably the best thing would be (while making
immediate arrangements for such actual work as is
required at once) to collect a few of the best people
in each country who have preferably had considerable
experience of international administration, and to
offer them temporary appointments during this summer
without determining their final position, and to associate them with the development of the organization
during the next few months.

PROPOSAL FOR A WORLD ECONOMIC CONFERENCE

Editor's Foreword

THIS paper of August 25, 1925, suggests a General Economic Conference. About ten days later, at the Sixth Assembly of the League in September 1925, Monsieur Loucheur (French Delegate) took up the suggestion and proposed that preparations for such a Conference should be set in hand: and the Assembly passed a resolution endorsing this. In December 1925 the Council set up a Preparatory Committee, which met in April and November 1926. An immense documentation was prepared.

The Economic Conference itself met in May 1927.

A PROPOSAL FOR A WORLD ECONOMIC CONFERENCE

August 25, 1925

The League has been frequently criticized for restricting its action within so much more modest limits in the economic, than in the financial, sphere. We have had an important, and very useful, Financial Conference. It has been urged that we should have followed this by an Economic Conference. We have undertaken, with success, ambitious schemes of financial reconstruction in Austria and in Hungary. It has been urged in both cases that we neglected unduly the economic side of the country's problem. In the economic sphere our action has been limited to such action as the very restricted Customs Formalities Convention, recommendations as to the Treatment of Foreigners, and similar work.

FINANCIAL AND ECONOMIC CONFERENCES

The reasons for the difference in the League's action in the two spheres may be briefly summarized as follows.

The establishment of a satisfactory financial system in different countries and in the world is eminently a matter for Governments, acting nationally and internationally, and so far as action extends beyond Governments, at least for *centralized* action. Governments alone can establish the essential conditions of a sound finan-

c

cial system—balanced budgets; and they alone, or they alone with a relatively small number of bankers and financiers, can establish sound currencies, and establish the institutions (banks of Issue with suitable constitutions), and the legislative basis necessary for their maintenance.

Economic reconstruction, on the other hand—the gradual repair and readjustment of production and of supply to demand, in every form of economic activity—is essentially the task of individuals, i.e. of manufacturers, merchants, and workmen. Governments can help and can hinder. But the main task is not theirs. (Incidentally it should be noted that if any action were contemplated, e.g. by a conference, this fact is important in determining the character and composition of the conference.)

Moreover, financial reconstruction claimed priority of attention because it is the indispensable prior condition, and *basis*, of economic reconstruction. No efforts of individual enterprise can achieve any stable economic results if the financial system, and therefore the medium of exchange, is liable to collapse underneath it.

Apart from these reasons for priority, it is evident that the difficulties of any agreement on principles of economic policy are enormously greater. In finance there was a general pre-war system, agreed and identical in its main principles. The great bulk of responsible opinion in almost all countries was agreed on the desirability of returning at least to the main principles of this system. With a fundamental agreement in objective, therefore, the discussions needed mainly concerned opportunity, practicability, and method. The divergences of economic policy, on the other hand, while intensified by war and post-war conditions, are rooted in much older controversies. There were fundamental differences as to the principles of tariff policy long before the war; and these differences are entangled with every sort of divergence of national and individual interest. And a discussion of economic policy not only raises questions of tariff policy but trenches upon such deep-rooted controversies as those on the relative merits of individual enterprise and public control.

The difference in the difficulties of agreement on financial and economic policy respectively is well illustrated by the financial and economic resolutions at the Conference of Genoa. The financial resolutions embody a coherent, logical, and detailed series of principles. The economic resolutions are so limited, tortuous, qualified by exceptions, and weakened by reserves as to be useless and almost unintelligible—in fact, perhaps worse than useless, as tending to crystallize and give some kind of international acceptance to a retrograde stage of world policy.

The considerations stated in the previous paragraph carry at least the following conclusions :—

(a) that the League has certainly been right *so far* in not convening a general economic conference of any kind;

(b) that neither now, nor in the near future, is a *general* economic conference, composed of *Government representatives*, likely to have any practical utility. Indeed, it might well do more harm than good. Conferences fully governmental in character must still be confined to special purposes, and limited to modest tasks, such as the Customs Formalities Conference of last year. (The view was held—and as the result has shown, rightly held—that even the Financial Conference had better not be fully governmental in character; and the reasons for this are much stronger in the case of an economic conference (see preceding paragraph).

It remains to be considered, however, whether the whole situation has not now so developed as to make a general economic conference in 1926 both practicable and desirable, so long as it is not fully governmental in character and does not aim at binding resolutions.

REASONS FOR AN ECONOMIC CONFERENCE

The case for such a conference, and for convening it in 1926, may be rapidly summarized as follows:—

Progress of Financial Reconstruction.—Financial reconstruction is nearing its completion. Seventy per cent. of the population of Europe have currencies linked with gold, as compared with 3 per cent. two years ago. The rest fluctuate within comparatively restricted limits, and efforts at achieving stability are well advanced. (No European exchange was, on its mean dollar rate, worse in January 1925 than January 1924 by as much as 5 per cent.) The great international obstacles to national financial reconstruction—an unsettled reparation debt and an unsettled inter-Allied debt—have been, or are well in the way of settlement for at least a considerable period. The only utterly disorganized exchanges—Austria, Hungary, Poland, Germany, Russia—are reformed and now on a gold basis. The need for international action is apparently at an end. The League has restored the smaller countries of Central Europe by its direct action and the rest by its example.

The *basis* of economic reconstruction is therefore attained or in sight of attainment.

Need for International Organizations.—But experience has shown that to provide private effort with a basis of economic recovery—the principle rightly adopted at the time by the League in Austria and Hungary, and the line of effort to which other international action was rightly subordinated—is not likely to be in itself sufficient.

It is significant that the League has just gone a step beyond its original plan in arranging an economic enquiry in Austria; and that Mr. Jeremiah Smith has just arranged a somewhat similar, though less formal, study of Hungarian economic conditions.

It has become clear that, if in the last resort economic reconstruction can only be achieved by individuals, their efforts may be rendered ineffective either by the economic policy of Governments, or by tendencies of policy and practice outside their individual control, *or* by world developments which can only be corrected or countered by collective action and agreement.

I would emphasize the latter alternative. Some of the causes of serious economic trouble are international in character, but do not arise from governmental action and can perhaps not be best dealt with by governmental or inter-governmental action. We have at the moment, for instance, the excess production of coal. It may well be that some form of international association or organization is desirable to deal with this and similar troubles. Such an organization (whilst international and including some representatives of workers and consumers as well as owners) might be unofficial, not governmental, in character. A general economic conference would doubtless discuss the practicability and desirability of such associations. It would be better fitted for this purpose if it were itself not fully governmental.

Advantages of Free Discussion.—There is reason to believe that many even of those who, if meeting as officials or Government representatives, would feel bound to take a line which would make any useful agreement impossible, would welcome a discussion from a more general point of view and under freer conditions. A politician or an official, in working out his economic policy, is bound to assume, as given factors in his problem, the existing policies of all other countries. The result may well be collective action which is regretted by all those who have contributed to it. An individual concerned with tariff policy is often in a position analogous to that of a depositor in a bank threatened by a panic among its investors. He may know that the bank is perfectly sound unless there is a run on it caused by panic, and that therefore a decision by all the individual investors to withdraw is collective insanity. But he may equally realize that to abstain from withdrawing himself may merely mean losing his own chance of getting his money without averting the ruin. All the depositors may think, and act, accordingly. The result of acts of individual prudence is collective insanity.

This is analogous to a good deal of the feeling among responsible people concerned with economic policy. The only beginning of a way out is some form of international conference, in which the individual tariff maker is as much concerned to criticize the policies of other countries as to frame his own.

The League's Responsibility.—The League has very definite duties in regard to economic policies. Article XXIII of the Covenant contemplates "equitable treatment" of the commerce of all members. However vaguely this may be expressed, it is certainly much more ambitious than anything which can be achieved solely by meetings of an official body like the Economic Committee, followed when practicable by official conferences like the Customs Formalities Conference. The League, itself a governmental institution, finds itself of necessity restricted by the hard limits set by the policies of its members. It is clear already that, within any near future, no substantial progress can be made on the present lines. This may indeed be inevitable, but the League has surely not done its duty until it has at least tried one method available to it of breaking out of the closed circle—i.e. the organization of a forum of general world opinion which may influence the policies of the Governments.

But quite apart from its specific obligations under Article XXIII, the League has the task, implicit in the whole of its duties, of trying so to influence the policies of the world as to increase the chances of the maintenance of peace. Now economic causes, beyond all question, are the most serious sources of possible future wars. For the future peace of the world probably the most important desideratum is that economic policy should so develop as to reduce future friction and conflict. The very principles of such policy have never yet been the subject of international discussion.

Public Opinion.—There is in any case such a strong and increasing feeling that the economic troubles of the world are in many of their aspects international in character, and should be at least discussed internationally, that a conference would be useful even in demonstrating the limits of practicable improvement by international action.

SCOPE OF THE CONFERENCE

What should be the scope and agenda of such a conference? These must depend upon the conception of its essential character and main object. The main conception, I think, should be that of a forum of responsible world opinion; and its object rather to pool, exchange, and publish opinion of this kind than to arrive at agreed resolutions and draw up a defined policy. The latter may be impossible; or if possible, may only be so at the expense of being useless by becoming platitudinous or positively pernicious. (The objections of a minority may either deprive agreed resolutions of all substance or even secure their drafting in a form which is more retrograde than the view of the majority.) Neither the agenda, therefore, nor the conduct of the discussions should be cramped in order to make it easier to secure agreed resolutions. Where the two interests conflict—that of securing the widest and fullest expression of responsible world opinion and that of securing agreed resolutions—the former should prevail. This should be made clear from the first, so that the conference may not be regarded as ineffective because it does not result in agreement.

With this preface, I think the scope of the Conference should be

(*a*) to obtain *exposés* of the actual economic situation in each country. These would set out, and estimate the relative importance of, the main obstacles to economic recovery, particularly as compared with the pre-war position. (This follows the precedent of the Financial Conference.)

(*b*) To discuss the principles and tendencies of economic policy likely to assist the economic recovery of the world; and to discuss possible action—whether official or private—likely to help to the same end;

(*c*) to discuss the principles and tendencies of policy likely to conduce to international amity and to reduce the dangers of economic conflicts threatening war.

Committee work—dividing the several main aspects of the general subject—would alternate with, and be followed by, general discussion at the main conference, as at the Financial Conference.

COMPOSITION OF THE CONFERENCE

The composition of the Conference should, I think, be somewhat as follows:—

(i) Each Government (including those outside, as well as in the League) should be asked to name members. Of these at least one should be a representative economist, and one a representative business man.

These members, while named by Governments—and their responsible character thus secured—would not be Government representatives.

This follows the precedent of the Financial Conference.

(ii) In addition, important institutions—whether economic or business—should be asked to name persons.

We have the precedent of the International Chamber of Commerce at the Customs Conference.

Persons so attending should be treated exactly as members under the first heading as to speaking, circulating documents, etc., but might be excluded from voting, if there is voting, or from certain of the votes.

(iii) As a special instance of appointment under (ii), it would be indispensable to arrange that the Labour movement is associated with the Conference.

(iv) Before the Conference was held, careful documentation would be prepared, as for the Financial Conference; and this documentation might well include the preparation of special memoranda by the chief economists, and spokesmen of international business, including those who would be unable to attend the conference.

VALUE OF A CONFERENCE

Such a conference will be adversely criticized as a mere talking-shop. It will be declared a failure, either because it will not reach conclusions, or because its conclusions are restricted and disappointing.

These criticisms were made both before and after the Brussels Conference. But looking back after five years, no responsible and intelligent person would deny the importance of its influence among the factors which have been restoring financial stability to the world. With every year that has passed its value has become more evident.

When, indeed, the League has tasks to fulfil, on which it can make no satisfactory progress within the limits of its normal official machinery, then a conference of this kind is the only practicable method of pioneering work. If based on official nomination, it is clearly within the rights and precedents of the League. At the same time, if it is non-governmental in the character of the mandates given to the delegates, it offers (as Brussels has shown) a most effective method of encouraging a world opinion which will influence and assist Governments in developing their policy—and which at a later stage will assist the League itself in consolidating the advance made in international conventions.

POSTSCRIPT

THE constitution and scope of the Conference followed closely the lines sketched in the paper.

As regards personnel, the members were drawn from fifty States, Members and non-Members of the League: some were nominated by the Governments, some were nominated by the Council or by organizations invited by the Council, and some were present as invited experts. None were Government representatives or spokesmen of official policy.

As regards agenda, the Conference had in view peace as well as prosperity: the Sixth Assembly, besides calling for investigation of "the economic difficulties which stand in the way of the revival of general prosperity," had declared that "economic peace will largely contribute to security among nations."

The Conference did reach agreement on precise and substantial Resolutions concerning commerce, industry, and agriculture. In particular it concluded that "tariffs, though within the sovereign jurisdiction of the separate States, are not a matter of purely domestic interest but greatly influence the trade of the world," and that "the time has come to put an end to the increase in tariffs and to move in the opposite direction"; it recommended "that nations should take steps forthwith to remove or diminish those tariff barriers that gravely hamper trade, starting with those which have been imposed to counteract the effects of disturbances arising out of the war," and "that in future the practice of putting into force, in advance of negotiations, excessive duties established for the purpose of bargaining, whether by means of *tarifs de combat* or by means of general tariffs, should be abandoned."   ED.

CHAPTER III

THE LEAGUE AND AMERICA

Editor's Foreword

THIS memorandum is self-explanatory. It was written early in the period of the Coolidge Administration, when it had become clear that, for some time to come, the attitude of America to the League was likely to be one of friendly detachment, with possibilities of gradual co-operation but not membership.

THE LEAGUE AND AMERICA

WRITTEN (EXACT DATE UNKNOWN) DURING THE EARLY
PART OF THE COOLIDGE PRESIDENCY

The recent definition and development of American
policy in relation to world affairs afford a firmer basis
than has hitherto been available for estimating the
future position and alternatives of the League.

It appears now to be clear (*a*) that America, under
its present administration, is irrevocably pledged
against direct association with the League as such,
(*b*) that she desires to take a part in world, and in
European, politics, and (*c*) that she would like to
take some action to render future war less probable,
if she can do so without inconsistency with her
pledges and her general policy with regard to the
League.

In these circumstances, those concerned in the
League have to consider whether they are to build
the League as a European League—at any rate, as a
League unsupported by America; or alternatively to
adopt a policy which in some form or another will
secure America's support.

So long as America's policy was undecided, I was
always in favour, after the first few months (when
America might have entered at any moment), of push-
ing straight on without reference to America. The best
hope of America's association during that period of
the formation of her policy lay in the League's claim to
respect for work done in the interval. The position is

very different, however, now that America's policy is definite.

If those who are interested in the League and in the objects for which the League was established, confine their attention to developing the League as it stands, I am afraid that the result will be that the League's secondary object will be secured, but that its main object will be lost.

The League has as its secondary object the assistance of international co-operation in the multitude of problems which since the war have an international character—the financial assistance of distressed countries, the regulation of exchanges, the co-ordination of railway systems, the repatriation of prisoners, the development of medical precautions against plague and infectious diseases, the improvement and standardization of labour conditions, etc. All these activities might be developed independently of America by the existing League working on its present lines.

But the first and overwhelmingly the most important object of the League was the preservation of peace. For this purpose a machinery of conciliation or arbitration and of judicial process is being established. I cannot but feel, however, that the whole of this part of the League's work will be rendered useless at The Hague if America's support is lacking. No machinery to try or settle disputes will be workable if there is no effective sanction which will persuade the disputants to place their case before the relevant tribunal. No such sanction exists or can exist without America for the more important cases. In relatively localized disputes, or disputes between very small countries, it is

possible that moral pressure by a few of the big countries would be sufficient, or that such countries would
even be prepared to detach a small body of troops,
which in the circumstances would be sufficient to
enforce their decision. Neither the one method nor the
other will be effective to make any of the major countries submit their disputes under the mechanism contemplated by the League. The only sanction which is
at once sufficient and practicable in such cases is the
sanction of economic boycott, but economic boycott
can never be possible if the strongest economic country
in the world is no party to it. What would be the
good of England and France trying to boycott a
country if it remained free to trade with America?
Moreover, what chance is there of persuading England
and France, in any circumstances, to enforce a boycott
in a quarrel not their own, against another country, if
the only effect of that boycott would be to turn over
their trade to America?

It seems to me, therefore, that the primary object of
the League can only be achieved if in some way or
another America's economic boycott is pledged in the
interests of a process of arbitration. There will obviously
be very great difficulties in securing this, and securing
it (which is essential) not only in fact when the dispute
matures, but as a menace sufficient to deter the disputants from taking a military action.

It is clear that America cannot and will not give
any such pledge in connection with the present
Covenant or the mechanism of the present League.
It appears to be clear, too, that she is in no circumstances likely to pledge in advance the use of her

economic boycott in support of future and unknown decisions of any tribunal. The actual issues which arise when war is threatened are so complex, the opportunities of intrigue with any tribunal so great, the difficulties of the representative of a distant Power in attempting to watch and discover such intrigues so insuperable, that America will undoubtedly decide that she must keep her hands free and be at liberty to judge the issue when it arises.

It is not, however, essential for the preservation of peace that the economic boycott of the world should be assured in support of the *award* of any tribunal. The great majority of wars would be avoided if a form of judicial and public enquiry were assured, together with time for the peoples of the disputing countries to learn, consider, and judge coolly the issues involved and the cost of war. This would be assured if the economic boycott were pledged not to support the *award* of a tribunal but only to enforce disputants to submit first to the process of enquiry by a tribunal before taking action; even though they still remain free to take aggressive action, without necessarily bringing the universal economic boycott upon them, and even in defiance of the award of that tribunal when its process of enquiry is completed and its award is announced. If only the *process* of arbitration were secured, it seems very doubtful whether any Government would in the present and probable temper of its people, and particularly of its working classes, be able to lead its people into war against the award of the tribunal after a period of reflection of from six months to a year.

America has always been in favour of the principle of arbitration, as an alternative if possible, and as a preliminary in all cases, to a settlement by war. It would be quite in accordance with her traditions and her policy, and not inconsistent with any political pledges she has recently taken, for her to pledge herself to use her economic boycott in common with the rest of the world against any country which took military action before having submitted its question to an arbitration tribunal. If the pledge were limited to this, it would avoid America's chief objections, which are, I understand, (*a*) to association with the League, and (*b*) to pledging herself to endorse the unknown award of a tribunal in which she may not have complete confidence.

In these circumstances, Republicans of influence who desire, while maintaining their pledges, to contribute towards world peace, might conceivably initiate a movement along the following lines :—

(*a*) America might invite *all* the Governments of the world, including both the signatories of the Treaty and other Powers, to a conference, to consider a simple universal pledge.

(*b*) She might propose that this pledge should be simply that every country would pledge itself to enforce an economic boycott against any country which began military action (including, of course, action by air and sea as well as by land) either without having previously offered to the country with whom the dispute had arisen to place issues before an impartial investigation commission or judicial tribunal, or after such an offer had been made and accepted. This pledge need not specify the nature of the commission or the tribunal. It would be sufficient in order to establish the *bona fides* of the offer that it should include a provision that if the nature of the tribunal could not be agreed between the disputing countries, some impartial authority (e.g. the Hague tribunal or the President of the United States) should nominate the relevant commission or tribunal. As to the character of the proceedings, it should be sufficient to require that they should be judicial in method, public and thorough. It would not even be necessary to provide for any central authority to determine whether the conditions had been satisfied. If the pledge were taken by every country, each country could itself determine whether the conditions had or had not been satisfied.

(*c*) If America took the initiative in proposing so limited a pledge, she might reasonably hope that it would be accepted not only by herself but by all the present signatories of the League, and by all the rest of the world, or all countries of importance.

(*d*) America might make it clear that while the universal world pledge would be limited in this way, she contemplated that any group of countries would be perfectly free to sign further commitments among themselves as they might wish; that is to say, the present League might continue with little or no modification as a League binding its present signatories. It might for special purposes well break up into smaller regional associations. For example, transportation problems which concern Europe scarcely need the association of South America for their consideration. At the same time, it might be recognized as in some loose way affiliated to the world union of all countries of which the basis was the single pledge.

Under such a system the League would find a driving force pressing disputants into its own machinery of the High Court of Justice, etc., though not exclusively into that machinery, and it would be able to proceed with its own European tasks. In the meantime the existence of the world pledge outside it would be an assurance of the process of arbitration and therefore probably of peace outside, as well as within, the scope of the League itself.

CHAPTER IV

THE ALTERNATIVE TO A REGIONAL LEAGUE

Development of Council Committee System. Development of Work affecting non-European Countries

OCTOBER 13, 1926

The absence of the United States of America, the unreality of the South American association, the withdrawal of Brazil and the ambiguous position of the Argentine, Bolivia, and Peru, the Monroe Doctrine and its effect in keeping away South American disputes, the condition of China, the general movement towards "European" consolidation, and other factors—have contributed to revive the idea of a "regional" League.[1]

In the form in which this is being advocated, it seems to me very dangerous and, indeed, disastrous.

For its primary task—the prevention of wars, especially great wars—the League must be universal. The causes of war extend beyond the range of any continent; the range of the war if it happens is likely to be world-wide; its consequences in any case affect every country; and the League's sanctions depend not only for their efficacy in operation, but for their deterrent effect on a hesitating aggressor, upon world-wide co-operation.

[1] Cf. Article in *The Round Table*, October 1926.—A. S.

It is of the utmost importance therefore to keep the framework of the League universal. It is better that the part which does not affect Europe should be a framework only than that it should be nothing.

But this will be difficult unless the framework can be gradually filled in with something—a mere shell is likely to collapse in time—and unless the machinery of a universal League can be so adjusted as not to be unduly cumbrous for the purely European tasks which must form for some time the bulk of the work of the League.

The problem of filling up the non-European framework is mainly a problem of (*a*) the United States of America, (*b*) South America, (*c*) the Far East.

The United States.—The United States of America has recently *receded*. The attitude to the Court, for example, shows a set-back as compared with the time when Coolidge first launched his policy. The response to the "reservations" Conference will indicate this. Had there been progress the answer would have been acceptable. As it is, America will probably not join the Court. The attitude of the Court was, however, certainly right. It maintains the position that we must make our League a workable organ, and must not damage its efficiency in order to sue for America's favour; but that, short of that, we will do what we can to facilitate America's co-operation. It gives the American advocates of entry the full advantage of the "reasonable" case, which they can make effective either now or later whenever the circumstances permit.

The reaction about the Court is only one of many

signs of the disastrous effect in America of the March fiasco.[1] The effect of Germany's entry, which should have offset this, has for the moment been largely discounted by the Council elections and new composition. If, however, the co-operation with Germany proves successful, the tide will doubtless begin to turn again. We shall have to watch opportunities, bearing in mind the following factors and principles:—

(i) Appealing to America to "come and help" does nothing but harm. America's approach will be in proportion to her respect for us, to her feeling that she can promote things she's interested in and can shape them more according to her own wishes and policy, and that she is losing by being left out.

The first condition of all this is that we should have self-respect and show it, that we should get on with our own job, and make our organization effective for our own problems.

(ii) While never beseeching America to come in for any particular task, we should, with an unvarying formal courtesy, make it clear that she would be welcome—that the door is always open.

(iii) We should *not* attempt to give America the advantages of membership without the responsibilities by trying to find out what is acceptable or not

[1] In March 1926 the Assembly met specially to admit Germany to the League, but owing to disagreement about the claims of Poland and Spain, Brazil, and Persia and China, to permanent seats on the Council, the Assembly had to be adjourned without Germany having been admitted. Germany entered the League in September; Brazil and then Spain gave notice of withdrawal; and a new plan was agreed on for semi-permanent seats on the Council.—ED.

acceptable and going on with the one and not the other.

For example, it has been suggested that we should announce that "immigration" would not be discussed at the Economic Conference because America wouldn't like it, and that such an announcement would increase the chances of her association with the Conference.[1] Quite the contrary. There may be other reasons for omitting this subject, but in framing the agenda we should exclude the consideration whether the subject is acceptable to her. She is more likely to come in if she is afraid of discussion than if what she might hope to obtain, or prevent, by association with the Conference is given or stopped without such association.

(iv) The real position of the present American Administration is on the whole *not*—"the League is damned" nor that it is "dead"; but that it is a useful organization for European affairs, and for certain world affairs in which America herself is interested. America should show a benevolent attitude to the former and participate as she finds desirable in the particular case in the latter. The acceptance of the political engagements is as far off as ever. The tasks in which co-operation is likely are such as disarmament and

[1] The World Economic Conference of May 1927, then in course of preparation. Immigration was not, in fact, included in the agenda of the Conference; but the documentation prepared for it included papers on population statistics, movement of population, migration, legislation on movement of labour, and on workers' standards of living; and the Conference made recommendations about the economic and fiscal treatment of nationals and companies of one country admitted to settle in the territory of another.—ED.

the whole range of technical and humanitarian work.

For the moment, America has receded a little from even this position, but she may be expected to come back to it. It is this line we should work along—and not complicate it with any thought in the near future of the political engagements.

In view of this we should:—

(i) Send polite, formal invitations (not accompanied by any form of appeal) to participate in such conferences as the Disarmament, Economic, etc.[1]

(ii) At the first sign of a more favourable attitude, proceed with a policy of inviting America to membership of technical bodies—Transit, Economic Committee, Financial Committee, etc.[2]

(iii) The next advance would be a declaration which would help the economic sanctions. What we

[1] In the year 1927 there were four world conferences called by the League: the United States was fully represented at all four. To the Economic Conference, the American Government, with the approval of Congress, sent thirty experts. To the Conference on Communications and Transit (at which Soviet Russia was not represented) the American Government sent a strong delegation of State, Commerce, and Shipping Board representatives. To the Import and Export Restrictions Conference the Government sent representatives of the State and Commerce Departments; and it authorized their signature of the resultant conventions. The Government also accepted for the first time an invitation to a disarmament meeting at Geneva, and was represented on the Preparatory Commission for the Disarmament Conference and the Conference on Arms Traffic.—ED.

[2] From 1927 onwards the United States has been represented on many of the League's Commissions and Committees, e.g. the Health Committee, Committee on Traffic in Women, and Protection of Children, Committees on Double Taxation, on Counterfeiting Currency, on Maritime Tonnage Measurement, on Opium, etc.—ED.

need is, not full co-operation—though we should like that—but a declaration that America would not interfere with our action. Coolidge could give such a declaration, in answer to an inspired question, in a form which would meet our primary need, without inconsistency with his policy and in a form in which repudiation or effective protest would be scarcely possible.

Asked as to America's attitude towards possible League sanctions he could say, "America is outside the League, and in no way bound by League decisions. She is entirely free to decide herself at the time whether or not she would in any way co-operate in any particular action to bring pressure on an aggressor State. She is, of course, interested in the success of any proper action to prevent aggression, and would generally therefore be in sympathy with League action if properly determined and applied. If the League decided upon a blockade, America might or might not be prepared to co-operate actively with it. But even in ordinary war, America, as a neutral, of course recognizes an effective blockade duly instituted in accordance with the principles of international law; and if such a blockade were instituted by countries acting in accordance with a League decision, she would equally recognize such a blockade and would, e.g., have no right to protest against the exclusion of American merchant ships from the blockaded area. This is no more than a statement of the existing position under international law. I need only add that, in the application of these principles, it is obvious that the general American attitude would be more favourable in the case of a blockade imposed by general decision of

League States against an aggressor than in the case of an ordinary blockade, in which there is no presumption that the blockading Power is more innocent than the blockaded."

The moment is not favourable for such a declaration. But it may come.[1] Such a declaration would certainly be the most useful help to us that is consistent with the main principle of America's policy. American Leaguers would make an effective campaign by showing that for the Government to protest against the exclusion of American supplies to a blockaded aggressor State is analogous to, but much worse than, the protest of a Government against American precautions against the smuggling in of alcohol. European countries, and particularly Great Britain, have gone very far in helping America in this problem: and "gun-running" is a worse crime than "rum-running."

Latin America.—The Latin American position is very difficult and dangerous. The successive withdrawals,[2] the increasing disposition to regard withdrawal as the natural retort to any decision that isn't liked, the ambitions and frictions, the injurious effect on League elections, the lesser interest which many of the questions naturally have for Latin America, and consequently the less representative character of the personnel, are in their cumulative effect very serious.

The presence of three Latin American States in a Council of fourteen, the character and position of

[1] Cf. Mr. Stimson's speech of August 8, 1932.—ED.
[2] Brazil had given notice of withdrawal a few months previously, in June 1926. Argentina had not been represented at League Assemblies since 1920.—ED.

these States, the method by which they were chosen
have all weakened the prestige of the League.

Three out of fourteen is a suitable proportion
even if all Latin America were effectively in, and even
if Latin American problems were being dealt with
as European problems are. Without either of these
conditions the proportion is excessive.

So far our efforts to attract Latin America have
been confined to:—

(i) Giving the places asked for, whether on Com
mittees or Council.

(ii) Constituting a Latin-American bureau.

This has brought a few Latin Americans to
Geneva. But it is not to be expected that this can
substantially affect the position in Latin America.

The problem is extremely difficult, but the following
factors may be taken into account:—

(i) There is, in the general work of the League as it
is at present, very little indeed that genuinely interests
Latin America.

Latin American countries don't so much fear war
between themselves. They know the ban of the Monroe
Doctrine against League intervention in American
disputes.[1] They don't fear the consequences of a

[1] The League Council did intervene in the Bolivian-Paraguayan
dispute on December 11, 1928, reminding the disputants of their
engagements in the Covenant, etc. The League took similar
action in 1932; and again in January 1933 in regard to a dispute
between Peru and Colombia. At the time when this paper was
written Latin American anxieties and susceptibilities about the
Monroe Doctrine were stimulated by the developments of United
States policy in Cuba, Nicaragua, and Mexico; and at the end
of the year feeling on the subject was further disturbed by publication of the United States-Panama Treaty of July 1926.—ED.

European war to themselves. The European questions treated rarely interest them.

These considerations largely explain Latin America's attitude, which in general is one of comparative indifference.

(ii) One of the factors which gives Latin American States an interest in League membership consists in their relations with the United States of America. They are not sorry to be members of an organization which may give some greater strength in their dealings with the United States of America, of whose suzerain predominance they are somewhat jealous. This is real, but cannot be pressed too far.

(iii) There *are* certain tasks which have some interest for Latin American States, and others which might have; for example, some questions of economic convention or legislation, and certain health questions.

We might do something to search out these questions and get them on our agenda. I have in mind such questions as legislation affecting development loans, the position and privileges of foreign capitalists, etc. In addition, the League might sometimes do the work which is so often done by American experts in a form in which North American influence and dominance develop. A country wants expert advice, for instance, in the reform of its finances, in the organization of a Customs service, in setting up a currency, etc. Such assistance now comes from North America. It might come through the League.[1]

There is another class of work that may have con-

[1] This was later done with health work in Bolivia and work in Brazil and elsewhere on leprosy, infant mortality, etc.—ED.

siderable possibilities. Latin American countries are still mostly in the stage of development in which "propaganda" forms a large part of their policy and outlook. They want, sometimes, to attract capital, sometimes to attract immigrants. They want media through which their resources and their requirements may be known. The League affords opportunities and might afford more. For example, the Minister in London of X recently saw me and discussed a possibility. He said X was undeveloped and had immense resources; its present population was only a small fraction of the population it could support. Good immigrants would be very valuable, i.e. the country had a real interest in doing the kind of work that the Dominions do in London in attracting immigrants through such organizations as their London offices. But X is poor; it can't spend a lot on advertising its resources; moreover, mere propaganda discounts itself. Could the League appoint competent experts who would visit the country, advise as to its best lines of development, publish a report which would show the world X's resources with an authority which would not attach to a body of persons appointed by the X Government itself?

Unhappily, the Minister was speaking without authority, and there have been no developments.

But this kind of work is work which the League might be suitably asked to undertake, and it might in some cases be of great value.

Obviously, such tasks can only be undertaken on the initiative of Latin American States. But obviously, too, a good deal of preparatory intermediate work would be necessary before any such initiative would be taken. The Latin Americans at Geneva, whether delegates or members of the Latin-American Bureau, *ought* to be doing such work as the main part of their occupation.

The method of beginning is not easy. But a visit of a good man, preferably knowing Latin America, but not necessarily a Latin American, to sound the position might be extremely valuable.

(iv) The Argentine is perhaps the crucial State. Its withdrawal was largely due to Germany's non-admission. Germany's influence might bring her back. And the others might follow.

Far East.—For the moment this is mainly the problem of China.

This is an even more difficult problem. Not only is China in dissolution, but the most general national sentiment is probably hatred of the foreigner (and incidentally the League, the foreigners' institution, so far as any one thinks of the League). The League can only approach China on a task which is not only of real benefit to China, but is recognized as such by the Chinese. League action must be positively wanted and not merely accepted.[1] Of the people who have hitherto come with proposals of League action, four out of five are people with property in, or claims on, China; and League action as envisaged by them would—whatever deceptive form may be proposed—in reality be a kind

---

[1] Between 1927 and 1931 the League was able to be of service to China in this way: it sent to China, at China's request, the Directors of the Health Section, the Transit and Communications Sections, etc., and Sir Arthur Salter himself.—ED.

of debt-collecting or of reassurance of foreigners' rights against the Chinese. This is hopeless. The only chance is an approach from the opposite end, e.g. the offer of League offices, at an appropriate time, to negotiate suitable reductions of certain foreigners' rights, e.g. the foreigner's right to limit China's power over her own customs.

Clearly the time is not ripe. We must watch for opportunities. We are trying to arrange for a valuable source of personal information, and we must be content, for the time, to watch and wait.

Russia.—To establish a contact with Russia is important both directly, and indirectly, as bearing upon the German problem, and on relations with the Far East. Directly, it is of special importance in connection with Disarmament, where little substantial progress can be expected while Russia is an unknown factor.

The obvious approach is through invitations to such bodies as the Preparatory Committees for the Economic Conference and the Disarmament Conference and, later, the Conferences themselves.

We invited Russians to join the first of these Committees. They accepted, and the Soviet Government agreed to their acceptance. They subsequently refused, however, to come to any meeting held at Geneva, because of the quarrel between Russia and the Swiss Government over the murder of the Russian representative at Lausanne. A similar position was taken in connection with Disarmament.

Thus a difficulty unconnected with the relations between the League and Russia has prevented an association that could otherwise have been established, and is likely to damage, perhaps fatally, a most important League conference.

This is really an intolerable position. It is obviously the wrong way to deal with it to hold meetings outside Geneva. We can't admit that the headquarters of the League is tainted ground. Moreover, there is no end to such a concession except the complete abandonment of Geneva.

The obvious solution is a settlement between Russia and Switzerland. So far, it has been treated as an affair affecting only the two Governments. But it is clear that it vitally affects the League. It seems to me essential that Members of the Council should discuss the question with Switzerland with a view to effecting a settlement, and this ought to be done at once.[1] Much harm has been done already, and the effect on Disarmament may well be fatal unless a way out of the impasse is found.

So much for the first part of the problem—putting reality into those parts of the League's universal framework which are at present empty and fragile. We now come to the second, i.e. the question of adjusting the League, with its world constitution, to the practical task of dealing efficiently with its mainly European problems. How shall we prevent the non-

[1] The impasse due to the murder of M. Vorovsky in Swiss territory was finally resolved in April 1927 through the good offices of the German Government. The Soviet Government then sent representatives to the World Economic Conference in May and to the Preparatory Commission on Disarmament in November 1927.—ED.

European "shell" encumbering and distorting our more local tasks?

The main answer, I think, lies in a considerable, elastic, and varying development of the *Council Committee system*.

Such a development is also desirable for two other reasons—the large size of the new Council, and the mass and bulk of detailed and often trivial work now dealt with directly by the Council.

As an illustration I may mention Danzig. There has probably never been anything more disproportionate in the history of the world than the amount of time and attention given by the representatives of ten States, including the Foreign Ministers of the Great Powers, to the domestic trivialities of a little town of less than 400,000 inhabitants.

I have in mind especially, not *ad hoc* Committees (though these, too, may be usefully developed) but standing Committees.

We have had a considerable experience of these. We have, for example—to take my own section—the *Austrian, Hungarian,* and *Greek* Committees of the Council.

These have been based on the following principles:—

(i) The membership consists of the three permanent European members, the country primarily interested and any others recognized as interested in the sense of Article IV and, therefore, members of the Council for the question.

Thus Great Britain, France, and Italy have been members of all three Committees.

The Austrian Committee has also included Austria and Czechoslovakia.

The Hungarian has included Hungary, Czechoslovakia, Roumania, and Jugoslavia.

The Greek has included Greece.

(ii) The Committees are only sub-committees and only advisory. They have no power to *vote*, even on questions on which the Council can take a decision by a majority.

(iii) In practice the Committees always receive in the first instance the reports of the responsible officer or bodies and of the relevant technical body (the Commissioner, or Commission, and the Financial Committee). They examine and approve, with or without modification, the recommendations. They discuss and arrive at agreement upon any political questions involved. They make recommendations to the Council, which in practice the Council has always adopted without more than formal discussion.

(iv) They have always met in secret.

This system has in fact been very efficient.

It has relieved the members of the Council not specially interested of a mass of detailed work.

The work has been rapid and efficient, with the advantages of a small and workable body, and of a simple and informal procedure in the meetings.

It has at the same time fully preserved the rights of the Council, as no decisions are effective except when taken by the Council itself. It is no derogation of this right that the Council has not had effective discussions and has not modified or disapproved recommendations. The knowledge that the Council had the ultimate right has always operated to keep the Committee discussions within what was felt to be the sense of the

Council. (For example, the termination of the Hungarian control was a matter to be decided in the Council by a majority: it could not be so decided in the Committee, where the majority would, in fact, very possibly have been different: the knowledge of the Council's ultimate right was effective in securing unanimity in the Committee.)

The retention of the right of decision by the Council is also an effective precaution against a specialized Committee taking a decision not acceptable to the rest of the Council, which, though in form of local application, might as a principle and precedent be of wider, or even of universal, application. The extension of such a system, with the retention of the essential safeguard that *decisions* can only be taken by the Council, would be a valuable contribution to the present problem.

Just in so far as the Committee was working with the general sense of the Council, its recommendations would be accepted, without taking the time of the Council except for formal and public exposition and explanation. Just in so far as a Committee might work outside its proper limits, and deal with principles of wider application, or be acting contrary to the wishes of other members of the Council, the real discussion would pass to the Council, whose time would then be engaged on such part of the work, and such only, as it was essential it should deal with.

The system could clearly be extended to Danzig questions, Minorities questions, the Saar, and doubtless many other special categories of problems.

But with a considerable extension, such as the new conditions require, it is doubtful whether all the principles mentioned above should be retained un-modified. Changes might well be made in two respects.

(i) The automatic inclusion of all the great European Powers, and no others except the "specially interested," is doubtful.

Germany is now a new Great Power on the Council. The inclusion of four Great Powers plus the interested Powers (who are sometimes as many as four, e.g. in matters affecting Hungary) might make the Committees too large. Perhaps some of the Great Powers might be represented on some committees and others on others. On the other hand, if the system is to be considerably extended, it might be well to have one Power to represent in the Committee the element which has been so important in the Council—viz. the "disinterested," as a mediatory element bringing un-biassed general world opinion to bear upon the particular problem. Such an inclusion would also increase the chances of later adoption of a Committee's recommendations by the Council.

(ii) With the withdrawal from effective primary discussion by the Council of some of the questions which now give life and reality to its meetings, there is a considerable danger of loss of public interest.

It might therefore be arranged that many of the Committee meetings should be in public.

Some extension and development of the Rapporteur system might also help. The work of the Rapporteur might often usefully be both more effective and con-tinuous. He might follow a subject right through, being normally a member of any Council Committee, and reporting not only to the Council but possibly also at the Committees of the Assembly. Such a development must obviously, however, vary very largely with the character of the subject and the qualities of the Rapporteur ; and the unequal qualities of different members of the Council must always mean that the development is both unequal and limited.

These are only intended as a few fragmentary and tentative suggestions bearing on the developments which the League must contemplate in the near future.

CHAPTER V

THREE COUNCILS OR FOUR?

Editor's Foreword

WHEN this paper was written, Sir Austen Chamberlain had lately (March 1927) proposed in the Council that the Council's annual sessions should be reduced from four to three. (The sequel is summarized in a Postscript.)

THREE COUNCILS OR FOUR?

April 5, 1927

If in the following paragraphs I am suggesting certain reasons for regretting the present movement for reducing the number of Council meetings, I wish at the outset to make it clear that I realize the strength of the arguments by which that movement is supported.

It is true that the Covenant does not provide for four meetings a year, and that its framers probably did not contemplate its meeting so frequently.

It is also true that during the years immediately following the war the League has had two classes of duties which naturally terminate or diminish with time, viz. settlement of questions left half-settled by the Peace Treaty, and questions arising from the unsettled conditions natural to the transitional period between war and a time of normal peaceful relations.

It is natural, too, that this progress towards normal peaceful relations should have been reflected in shorter and less important Council agenda for recent meetings.

Moreover, I fully recognize the enormous advantage to the League of the habitual attendance at the Council of Foreign Ministers, especially of the Great Powers.[1] This has been one of the main causes, and expressions, of the advance made by the League in the last few years. If it were a choice between three meetings with

[1] This began in 1925, when Sir Austen Chamberlain made a practice of habitual attendance.—Ed.

Foreign Ministers and four without, I agree that the case for the reduction would be decisive.

There are, however, I think, some important qualifications of these arguments to be made.

Till recently, Council agenda were normally overloaded and more than four meetings would have been desirable. With the recent reduction, the work just about falls reasonably within the compass of a week. And the normal results of a week can scarcely be said to be disproportionate to the time of the members involved. During the last meeting, e.g. the Saar dispute, the Silesian dispute, the Estonian and Danzig loans, the Traffic in Women Report, when added to minor decisions essential to the progress of a maze of current work of committees, etc., make a respectable total. When there is added to this the value of unofficial discussions and negotiations (such as those between Poland and Germany)—a general aspect of the problem which is developed below—the week was surely well worth while.

Surely it is premature to assume that the retention of four meetings means losing the presence of the Foreign Ministers. There are at present certain purely temporary factors which help to make them feel that four journeys is an excessive toll on their time. Just now the British Foreign Minister is, of course, mainly preoccupied with the Chinese question,[1] which is

[1] At this time the whole of China was in a state of civil war between the Kuomintang and a coalition of Northern War Lords; outrages against foreigners had lately been committed in Nanking: Kuomintang forces were fighting Communists at Shanghai, outside the foreign settlements, and the British Defence Force at

neither a League question nor one on which conversations at Geneva were last month likely to be of special value. In the latter respect at least it is an exception among important international questions—and even China may not continue to be such an exception. Similarly there were special, and probably temporary, considerations also in the minds of M. Briand and Herr Stresemann in addition to those of more permanent importance. Sometimes doubtless a Foreign Minister will be unable to attend one or other of four meetings. This may, however, apply even to one of three; and if he can attend only three in a year, surely three attendances of Foreign Ministers plus one of a substitute is not necessarily worse than three attendances only.

And if it is true that the framers of the Covenant did not contemplate four Council meetings a year, it is probable that they had not foreseen (a) the volume and extent of the League's work of international co-operation (as distinct from settlement of disputes), and (b) the advantage of Geneva meetings for unofficial discussions and negotiations.

Against the arguments for change as stated and qualified above, there are certain very definite disadvantages :—

(a) In particular classes of work the longer interval before authority can be obtained may involve real disadvantage.

As regards the work of *financial reconstruction*, for example, the longer intervals would certainly have been

Shanghai was being reinforced. An agreement between Britain and the Kuomintang Government had lately been negotiated for the rendition of the British Concession at Hankow.—ED.

prejudicial to the work. Normally, the Financial Committee meets four time a year, just before the Council; and normally its recommendations require urgent action for which Council approval is necessary. Under a three-Council system, no loan not ripe for approval before the first part of May could be issued before October; and the difference might well be of decisive importance. Moreover, the system of quarterly reports from Greece and Bulgaria, adjusted to the meetings of the Committee and Council, would presumably be changed; and quarterly supervision is substantially more satisfactory.

(b) The interval of, on an average, nearly four months instead of nearly three increases the danger in respect of international complications which are not obviously and demonstrably of such urgency and importance as to secure a special meeting. And the temptation in certain cases to choose a date just after a Council meeting, to initiate some action which would have been discussed, unofficially or officially, if it had been taken shortly before or during a Council meeting, is increased if the prospective period before the next meeting is longer.

I do not think that we can rely on getting special meetings except when the danger of war is both obvious and imminent. When the situation is developing towards the point of obvious danger, but has not yet quite reached it—i.e. is at precisely the stage when it could best be dealt with by international discussion—it will be very difficult to secure a special Council meeting. The difficulty will be greater now that there are fourteen members to assemble. The meeting being, *ex*

hypothesi, unexpected by the members, other engagements will conflict. As a special meeting, it will adver-
tise the gravity of the crisis and by some, therefore, be
thought to increase it. It will not give the opportunity,
as an ordinary Council would, for unofficial treatment
without formal Council discussion, which may often
be the best method. In these circumstances, in the
class of case I have in mind, a special meeting will be
very difficult, and I think impossible wherever an
influential member of the Council is interested in
preventing it.

(*c*) I assume M. Comert[1] will be reporting as to
publicity—from the point of view of the invaluable
system of resident journalists, of immediate Press
publicity, of the whole mechanism of external private
propaganda, etc. All would be considerably reduced—a
very great loss during the period, far from finished,
when the League is building up its essential basis of
sustained, active, and informed public opinion.

But more important than any of these short-view
considerations, is the fundamental conception of the
international rôle of the Council, the League, and
Geneva.

My own personal conception of this rôle may be
briefly summarized as follows. It should include:—

(*a*) *Settlement of differences, not involving immediate danger
of hostilities, conclusion of "peace treaty" tasks, etc.*—These
have formed, perhaps, the greater part of Council
Agenda hitherto. They should considerably diminish.

[1] M. Pierre Comert, Head of the Publicity Section of the League
Secretariat till 1933.—ED.

(b) *Settlement of "dangerous" disputes.*—These are liable to happen at any moment; they should be less frequent, and can be partly met by special meetings—but subject to the important remark in (b) of the previous section.

(c) *Development of positive work of international co-operation in every sphere.*—This should be *continuously* increasing and developing; and should mean normally as much extra work for the Council as will offset reductions under (a) and (b).

This involves, it is true, some increase in the range of subjects which have hitherto occupied no substantial part of a Foreign Minister's time; but it is one which corresponds to a very real development in the world's affairs.

(d) Above all, Geneva should—at periods of the Council and the Assembly—offer the *normal* method by which international contact is effected.

By "contact" I do not of course mean the great mass of work which occupies the greater part of the time of a Foreign Office, and a very substantial part of that of a Foreign Minister. Policy must continue to be worked out in its detail; many conventions must be drafted; urgent questions arising in the intervals of even quarterly meetings must be dealt with; negotiations with countries not members of the League, or not represented (like some non-Council States) at Geneva during Council meetings, or not effectively represented (like China), must throughout be conducted outside Geneva.

I mean only the "contact" which secures the general basis of understanding on which the relations between countries are built up; the conversations and discussions which establish the atmosphere, the outline, and the *general lines or principles* on which negotiations will afterwards proceed; and I have in mind, of course, only contact between those countries which are, or may well be, effectively represented at Geneva. (I am not thinking, for example, of contact with non-Council States who are represented, at times of Council meetings, not by Members of the Government but by resident Ministers or officials.) And I have in mind the kind of discussions which a Foreign Minister will be prepared to undertake with the assistance of only a few of his principal officials, not those which would involve the attendance of a great number.

But the conception I have in mind does imply that, for the limited but very important work I have described, the direct contact of Foreign Ministers, each attended by some of his responsible officials, at a common neutral meeting ground and at regular periodical meetings, has such decisive advantages that it ought to be secured wherever practicable.

The system of contact through interviews with foreign Ambassadors and Ministers in the national capital, together with despatches from national Legations abroad, would, of course, still be the only method practicable in a large number of negotiations, and, even where negotiations have been initiated at Geneva, would be necessary to supplement them. But for establishing the basis of understanding the direct personal contact clearly has great advantages. Similarly, too, contact at regular periods has great advantages over specially improvised meetings between

Foreign Ministers, in avoiding the difficulties attendant upon the special public excitement which is often aroused by such special meetings. In contrast with the anxiety often caused by such special meetings, the public has, I think, come to derive a sense of security from the knowledge that Foreign Ministers are meeting frequently and regularly at Geneva.

If this conception is definitely adopted, with all its implications, much follows. As an example, I recently asked the Foreign Minister of a non-Council member whether he intended to be at Geneva during the next Council meeting. He replied, "Certainly, and whether my country has any question before the Council, or not; for where else can I in a few days secure direct, personal, and effective contact with the Foreign Ministers of the chief countries of Europe? If I stay at home I deal at second hand. If I travel to one capital, my visit excites public comment, and I have a formal interview with one Foreign Minister. At Geneva, at the expense of one journey and without public excitement, I have a more personal contact with several."

I need not emphasize further the developments that might follow from the growing adoption of this point of view. But on this conception of the method of diplomacy to which the world should move, is it excessive to contemplate four meetings a year? Let me put it this way.

A Foreign Minister's task is to relate the policy of his own country to that of all other countries. Half of his task is to express and persuade his own Parliament and people; half, to understand and influence the policies of other countries. If he can do (at a reasonable estimate) half of the second part of his task by conversations at Geneva, is four meetings, or six weeks of his time, an excessive price to pay?

I feel convinced that, if only Foreign Ministers would continue their quarterly attendances, the advantages of this method of adjusting the main lines of international policy would both increase and be more fully appreciated. A reduction to three meetings, on the other hand, would necessarily tend to make the method of indirect contact more normal. The mere increase in the interval will itself result in questions which could have been more effectively discussed at Geneva being dealt with elsewhere. And the movement once started may not stop. Some questions which have fallen outside the Geneva orbit through the longer intervals will in time constitute a pull towards the national capitals, which in turn will later suggest a further saving of time for work at home by a further reduction of Council meetings, and so on.

We are now at a point of unstable equilibrium. If we can hold on, the work naturally done at Geneva will grow up to the full opportunities of four meetings. If we start reducing, we shall set in movement a diversion of work which will later force further reductions.

Lastly I would like to add a few remarks as to the effect on public opinion.

The first impression will certainly be that the decision indicates at least a retarding of the League's progress; and probably that it expresses a desire both to retard progress and to restrict present functions.

And, however unjustly, it will certainly, in the public mind, be set in the series of initiatives taken by the present British Government all suggesting the same attitude—the rejection of the Protocol (and the reasons by which the rejection was justified), the criticism of the Mandate questionnaire (interpreted as a desire to make Mandate supervision unreal), the "competence" resolution,[1] and the attitude towards limitation of the League's budget.

And, apart from such a suggestion of restriction of function, the decision will tend to suggest a further movement in the direction of the control of League mechanism by the Great Powers and the choice or disregard of that mechanism at their own convenience and with little regard for the rights and wishes of the smaller Powers.

[1] I.e. Council Resolution of July 1926, proposed by Sir A. Chamberlain, arising out of the report of the Child Welfare Committee. The British Government held that some of the subjects dealt with in the Report did not call for international regulation, and the Committee was urged to keep strictly within "the limits of its competence."—ED.

POSTSCRIPT

SIR AUSTEN CHAMBERLAIN'S suggestion that the number of regular Council Meetings should be reduced from four to three met with much criticism. In June 1927 Sir Austen Chamberlain (who in 1925 had set the example of regular attendances as Foreign Minister at the Council) replied that the presence of so many responsible Ministers had increased the authority of the Council, but that it was "very difficult for Ministers of Foreign Affairs to leave their posts four times a year to attend meetings at Geneva, and it might therefore become necessary for them, if four annual sessions were held, to nominate others to take their places at the Council table."

Opposition to the proposal was maintained at the Eighth Assembly, on the ground that it would retard the League's working.

In December 1927 the Secretary-General stated that "from the administrative point of view, a reduction in the number of annual sessions to three would not hurt the work of the League": on the more important political aspect he did not wish to express an opinion.

Finally, in September 1929 (Mr. Henderson being then the British Foreign Secretary), the Council decided to reduce its annual sessions from four to three.

An additional reason for this decision was that by this time the control of the League's finances had been taken over by the Assembly. Hitherto the League's annual budget had been placed on the Council's agenda at each June session. At the end of 1929 the Council abandoned its June session, and substituted for the meetings in December, March, June, and September, meetings in January, May, and September. There have, however, been special meetings and prolonged sessions of ordinary meetings which have to a substantial extent filled the gap.—ED.

CHAPTER VI

THE "UNITED STATES OF EUROPE" IDEA

Editor's Foreword

IN the summer before this paper was written there had
been considerable discussion of the idea of a United States
of Europe. The idea had been put forward in 1923 by
Count Coudenhove-Kalergi in his book, *Pan-Europa*, had
been supported by M. Herriot in October 1924, and
January 1925, and had been favourably regarded by
Dr. Stresemann.

Then, by the end of August 1929, it became known
that M. Briand was likely to make a speech at the Tenth
Assembly, encouraging the idea. It was in these circumstances that the following paper was written, and distributed privately amongst those interested on September 2nd.

On September 5th M. Briand's speech in the Assembly
indicated support of the idea: and on September 9th, at
a luncheon given by M. Briand to the representatives of
the twenty-six European States Members of the League
(besides France), he spoke explicitly in favour of some
kind of European Federal Union.

At the request of this gathering M. Briand prepared the
memorandum which is the subject of Chapter VII.

THE "UNITED STATES OF EUROPE" IDEA

The World Economic Conference of 1927 demonstrated beyond question the existence of a general, indeed universal, dissatisfaction with the tariff systems as they now exist.

This dissatisfaction was due largely to the increase in level, complication, and instability of post-war tariffs, and to the fact that the war has created new tariff-making authorities and therefore smaller economic units.

It was due, however, to one other fact which it is well to emphasize, viz. that the natural development of industry towards large-scale operations is constantly increasing the handicap of small economic units. Trade barriers are not only therefore worse absolutely than before the war; but their obstructive effect on natural economic development is also greater because the advantages of development on a basis of equal opportunity in large markets are constantly increasing.

The policy recommended by the Conference under these conditions was the general and undiscriminating reduction of tariffs, together with their simplification and stabilization. The method contemplated was threefold :—

(*a*) Unilateral action—each country acting independently in the hope or with the example of other countries doing the same.

(b) Bilateral action—pairs of countries negotiating reductions on articles of special interest to themselves and extending the advantages of these reductions to other countries by virtue of the unconditional Most-Favoured Nation Clause.

(c) Multilateral action—collective agreements being negotiated for the simultaneous removal of barriers and reduction of tariffs.

The result after two years, as recognized by the Economic Consultative Committee of May last, may be briefly summarized.

The first method (unilateral action) had substantial immediate success in arresting what had hitherto been a rapid upward movement. Largely under the influence of the forces revealed and made effective by the Conference, projects involving large tariff increases were dropped or amended; and new demands for such tariffs were discouraged. Some, though not many, actual reductions on tariffs in force were also made. Since 1927 this influence on unilateral action has become less; it has not secured any general downward movement and on the whole recent increases have perhaps been more important than reductions.

The second method, bilateral action, also had a considerable success in 1927 ("the year of commercial treaties"), numerous and substantial reductions being negotiated and extended by virtue of the Most-Favoured Nation (M.F.N.) clause. After the accomplishment of 1927 it was, of course, not to be expected that there would be an equal advance in 1928, but even allowing for this, the record of bilateral treaties in 1928 was disappointing; the treaties of that year do not usually include tariff reductions, and are often designed to secure liberty to make increases; and this method shows no sign of giving satisfactory results now.

Multilateral action has had notable successes (subject to conventions which have been signed being ratified) as regards trade barriers other than tariffs (prohibitions, etc.); and constituted the most notable feature of 1928. But, except in the very limited and special case of "skins and bones,"[1] it has not touched tariffs.

On the whole the general situation is not very substantially either better or worse than in 1927; trade barriers other than tariffs being less, but tariffs on balance somewhat higher. The upward movement has been more or less—but even that not certainly—arrested. It has not been reversed.

The causes of this almost stationary—and certainly not satisfactory—situation are numerous.

All the trade barriers which the Conference sought to remove are of course buttressed by some private interest which has developed business under its protection.

These private interests are better organized, more vocal, and more politically effective, than the general public interests on the other side; and are much more conscious of what they would stand to lose than the other business interests (such as exporting industries) of what they would gain. Exporters and industries which would certainly gain by a reduction in tariffs, even those of their own country, have been disappointingly

[1] Convention against import and export prohibitions.—ED.

indifferent when their support might have been decisive.

In these circumstances unilateral action has been very difficult, each country finding it politically impossible to reduce its tariffs without some assurance that other countries would do the same, and the belief in such general, though independent, action waning with the lapse of time during which no country took a decisive lead. The one great country which had given such a lead in the past was, for various political and other reasons, not in a position to do so in the first two years after the Conference.[1] Multilateral action, in view of the enormous complexity of different systems and the differences of national situations and traditions, and the absence of a strong enough world impetus to reduce, has been deemed impossible. Bilateral action of a tariff-reducing character has also been arrested for reasons which merit special consideration; and one in particular—the operation of the unconditional M.F.N. clause under existing conditions.

The unconditional M.F.N., long the traditional basis of British policy, now claimed by the United States of America, and accepted to an increasing extent by Continental nations accustomed to the principle of reciprocity, may claim great advantages. It is designed to secure equality and undiscriminating treatment, simplicity, and the avoidance of dangerous complications and confusions of political and economic motives; and thus the avoidance of many causes of friction.

The two principles, "reciprocity" and "no dis-

[1] Great Britain between 1927 and 1929.—ED.

crimination," logically alternatives, are in practice
capable of conciliation under certain conditions. A
country giving and claiming undiscriminating treatment can without difficulty secure what it asks from
countries which negotiate reciprocal treaties *inter se*,
if it is a free-trade or a low-tariff country. Two countries arranging reductions of special interest to each
other are content to give the advantage to other
countries if the latter's general policy is such as not to
make the resulting situation impossibly unfair. Even
though the duties are equal for other countries, the
choice of the articles by the two negotiating countries
gives the "reciprocity" principle a real sphere of
action. But when countries whose principle of policy
forbids them either to give or accept differences in
tariffs have high tariff systems, the situation rapidly
becomes impossible. When two moderate tariff countries can only negotiate reductions *inter se* if they are
prepared to give these reductions to countries whose
general tariff is higher than even their unreduced
tariff and who give them no advantage in return, two
results will follow: first, reduction by the method
of bilateral agreements extended by M.F.N. will be
arrested (this we have seen in 1928); and secondly
there will be a growing feeling that some modification
in the unconditional M.F.N. is both just and necessary.

The American tariff has forced this difficulty into
great prominence; and it has been aggravated by other
factors. The United States of America has become the
greatest exporter, not only in total but also of industrial
products. She has within her own frontiers the greatest

natural resources and the biggest consuming market in the world. Every manufacturer can organize his business with the knowledge that over the whole of this market no competitor can enjoy an advantage over himself; he can therefore develop methods of standardization and large-scale operation impossible to those who have a similar security only as regards a much more limited market. With this advantage he can export abroad with a special advantage over competitors in other countries. The United States of America, moreover, has one of the highest tariff systems in the world, and is increasing it. On the top of this, the United States of America is one of the two largest creditors—far the largest as regards public debts; and therefore presents herself to the world as refusing to take the goods with which other countries can alone ultimately pay them. She is succeeding in at once having more exports than imports and drawing large cash payments in respect of debts. The only possible result is an increasing American capital investment, in one form or another, in other countries. And to many countries this presents the aspect of increasing financial, and indeed political, domination.

In these circumstances it is intelligible, though regrettable, that the problem considered by the Conference of 1927—viz. "how to increase world prosperity"—has been gradually, in the public mind, taking another form, viz. "how can Europe compete against America?"

As to the strength of this development there can be no question. In France, in Germany, in Spain, in Czechoslovakia, the evidence as regards not only public opinion, but also official opinion, is overwhelming for something that is usually called the "United States of Europe." Strong, however, as is the feeling behind such a conception, it is difficult to obtain any clear and precise definition of it. What emerges clearly is, however, that the conception usually assumes an anti-American form.

This is regrettable for many reasons. The American progress may positively injure certain special industries, especially some which are particularly conspicuous, such as the motor industry, in Europe. But it does not diminish European prosperity *absolutely*: it increases it. The investment of American capital in Europe has many advantages, and its dangers are greatly exaggerated. Moreover, an attempt to meet the situation by any other method than that of increasing efficiency, and establishing the conditions that favour it, is at once doomed to failure and fraught with great political and other dangers. For every reason the positive and constructive approach—"how enable production and therefore prosperity to be increased by securing the necessary conditions"—is the right one.

We are thus faced with the following position. Progress solely upon the lines recommended by the Economic Conference has been arrested. Partly due to disappointment with this, partly to other causes, we have the development of a strong force which, in one aspect, presses towards the removal of trade barriers, and, in the other, contemplates discrimination* in tariffs. It is at once capable of much good and fraught with certain dangers. It is too strong to ignore, and perhaps too strong to defeat. And even if the force were defeated, the process of defeat might involve the waste of a force that might have been turned to a good use. The very fluidity of the idea, and the absence of a definite programme, give an opportunity. How can this be used?

First, what does the conception of a United States of Europe mean to those who use the phrase?

Its obvious meaning is complete free trade within Europe: a Zollverein of the countries of Europe. But can it be seriously believed that this is a conception that has any practicable chance of realization as an economic policy only, and in the absence of very great political changes? Zollvereins have been often preached, not infrequently attempted, but *never*, I think, realized, except under the conditions of an overwhelming political motive and an extremely close political association between the countries concerned. A consideration of the principal factors involved will explain this.

A Zollverein means a common tariff, which involves a political instrument to determine it; it means the distribution of the proceeds to all the member States, and again therefore a political instrument to determine how the distribution should be made. The commercial and tariff policy of European States is so central and crucial a part of their general policy, the receipts from Customs are so central and substantial a part of their revenues, that a common political authority, deciding for all Europe what tariffs should be imposed and how they should be distributed, would be for every country almost as important as, or even more important than, the national Governments, and would in effect reduce the latter to the status of municipal authorities.

In other words, the United States of Europe must be a political reality or it cannot be an economic one. This consideration is so fundamental that it seems hardly worth emphasizing the fact that the main competition of every country in Europe is not with America but with other European countries; that it was this competition and not American which was the origin of the tariffs; and that, if the American competition and tariffs are an additional obstacle to their removal, as they are, they are not the only one.

The main conclusion seems certain—that, in any reasonably near future and in the absence of a political development which would be little short of a political federation of Europe, no European Zollverein in the full sense is conceivable.

What, then, remains? There remains the possibility of an association or associations between countries, in or out of Europe, for the purpose of arranging by common agreement for lower tariffs *inter se* than with the rest of the world, or some part of the rest of the world.

Whatever form such association might take, it involves as an essential and indispensable factor the acceptance of the principle that a country may impose different duties on the same class of article according to the country from which it is imported, i.e. the principle of discrimination which it is the object of the M.F.N. policy to abolish.

Any such proposals may, therefore, be condemned in some quarters as both retrograde and dangerous.

Retrograde, because great progress has recently been made in the acceptance of the principle of unconditional M.F.N. (before the War by the United States of America, and since then by France and other countries, so that the inclusion of such a clause is now a normal feature of commercial treaties). The World Economic Conference has exerted its influence in this direction, and this has been followed up by the Economic Consultative Committee and the Economic Committee.

Dangerous, because discrimination is a fruitful source of friction; and also because it might easily become the basis, not so much of reduction but of a new upward competition of tariffs. It would, for example, be perhaps politically easier for European countries to retain otherwise their present tariffs and add on a certain percentage against non-European, or some non-European, countries than to agree upon reductions applicable to all except such countries. The dangers of resentment and retaliation on the part of the countries discriminated against, and of political friction, are obvious.

At the same time, before the idea is summarily dismissed, it is necessary to weigh some very important considerations on the other side.

It is true that the acceptance, in principle, of the unconditional M.F.N. clause has made great progress. But it is also true that that is now seriously threatened, most notably but not solely by the increased American tariff. Moreover, the practical effect of the clause can be, and often is, in practice largely destroyed by various devices of classification, nomenclature, restriction, etc. . . . In addition, the necessity of including the clause operates, as explained above, as an obstacle to reduction of duties by bilateral agreement.

Moreover, the application of the clause in its fullest sense, and without any exception whatever, cuts away the very basis on which multilateral conventions are negotiated. Why should a country attend a Conference and subject itself to the process of reciprocal concession if, by standing outside, it can without obligations to itself enjoy the full fruits of a convention made by the concessions of others? The Imports and Exports Prohibitions Convention may be cited as an instance of this.

The Economic Committee has recognized this difficulty, and devoted a great deal of attention to the subject, with the result that it agrees that a "reservation in plurilateral conventions may appear in some cases legitimate," but that "it can only be justified in the case of plurilateral conventions of a general character and aiming at the improvement of economic relations between peoples."

This exception was probably not intended, at least not intended by all the members, to cover such proposals as are now under consideration; but it contains a principle which may possibly be useful in examining them, and may well be taken as a starting point.

We must also face seriously the great difficulties in the way of securing reduction of tariffs by methods which exclude altogether any discrimination.

We have tried for two years the methods contemplated by the Economic Conference, with the results summarized above.

If general and undiscriminating reduction gives no satisfactory results, the only alternative method is working up to it by more local and geographically restricted action which, by definition, implies at least temporary discrimination.

Under the existing doctrine this can only be done in two ways. First, local Zollvereins (in the full sense), can be created; they do not involve a breach in M.F.N. clauses. Some such agreements have been attempted, e.g. Latvia and Estonia; but none have succeeded. The reasons given on pages 91 and 92 show why it is unlikely that any success, or any beyond the most narrow limits and in exceptional circumstances, will be achieved.

Secondly, in special cases agreement might be negotiated, not only between the countries to be directly associated, but those against whom the higher tariff would operate. An attempt was made in the Treaty of St. Germain to secure a temporary arrangement applying to the new Succession States. It was a dead letter. A prolonged attempt was made to revive it later, in connection with the special economic troubles of Austria. This also failed, after giving a vivid and convincing illustration of the difficulties of this method.

There remains no method for the League to advocate except that which involves, in some form or another, the acceptance of the principle that some countries may, under certain conditions, properly refuse, with the support of League authority, the application of the unconditional M.F.N. as at present framed and interpreted.

We must therefore examine whether there are any conditions which could, without rendering effective concerted reduction by this method impossible, so reduce the dangers as to justify the League in supporting such a policy.

The best method will be to try to imagine a scheme, with such safeguarding conditions, and the steps by which we might attempt to work towards it.

Such an attempt is made below, not with the object of advocating the adoption of a particular scheme, but in order to afford a concrete basis for considering whether working towards the removal of barriers by some form of local grouping is practicable and desirable; and whether, therefore, the League should encourage a procedure leading to that end.

As each feature, or condition, or step in procedure, is mentioned, the reader can ask himself: "Is this practicable?" "What dangers is it intended to avert?" And at the end he will perhaps be in a better position to judge whether it is desirable to take the first step.

Subject to this, let us imagine the following procedure.

Procedure.—The proposal might be launched on the highest political plane by speeches at an Assembly of the League, e.g. by M. Briand responded to by Herr Stresemann, and presented from the first as a counterpart of, and a contribution to, a developing political *rapprochement.* Such speeches would doubtless not include anything in the nature of a scheme. But they might suggest some of the principles noted above as averting or mitigating some of the worst dangers and suspicions.

Resolutions might follow, instructing the Economic Organization—in view of the natural tendency of industry to develop on a basis of large-scale production, which requires secure and free entry into large market, and of the consequent handicap to smaller economic units—to consider the best practical measures for the enlargement of these units; and to prepare the basis for a general conference to be held, by a date to be specified, for the adoption of such measures.

This approach has the advantage of suggesting the constructive and inoffensive aspect of the conception. Its defect is that it is too vague. Somewhat less vague, but also rather less inoffensive, would be such a formula as "to examine the special difficulties that arise from the great difference in size and importance of existing economic units and to consider the best practical measures for overcoming them"; and the rest as before.

This procedure is, however, not enough in itself; for any proposals involving such a transformation in the political conception and commercial policies of European countries, a procedure which included from the first, and at appropriate stages throughout, the actual political forces of the countries concerned, would be essential.

Responsible, authoritative, but unofficial opinion has shown its power, and the limits of its powers, at the World Economic Conference. The Economic Consultative Committee continues its work with the same kind of advantages and limits. The Economic Committee, in view of its composition, incorporates official authority (in fact if not in form) within the limits of such major conceptions of policy as exist, but it is incapable by itself of transforming them. While therefore a great part of the work of preparation can be done by the existing authorities, it will be necessary to supplement those authorities, during the period of preparation, by the association of the actual responsible Ministers (sometimes the Ministers of Commerce, sometimes the Ministers of Agriculture, but sometimes also the Foreign Ministers or even the Prime Ministers, or some combination of these); and the Conference itself must not take place until these preliminary meetings offer a prospect of success, whether upon the lines of the above conception or upon others.

If these meetings should demonstrate the impracticability of any such conception, they may by that very fact prepare the way for practical and effective action along the lines contemplated by the World Economic Conference.

But whatever the ultimate solution, experience suggests the extreme improbability of results being secured until the appropriate Ministers (including the Ministers of Commerce, but not these alone) are brought into as direct and regular contact with international economic problems and with each other as Foreign Ministers are within the purely political sphere.

It will now be well, subject to the remarks above, to try to imagine the kind of scheme which might emerge.

SCHEME SUGGESTED FOR DISCUSSION

The motivation might be that, "in view of the natural tendency of industry to develop on a basis of large-scale production which cannot be organized except with secure and equal opportunity in markets much larger than those comprised within the political frontiers of many or most States, the contracting States desire to remove the obstacles which at present obstruct such natural development by concerted action; with this object they are forming an association to promote greater and freer economic intercourse, and to secure the substantial, progressive, and if possible complete removal of economic barriers *inter se*."

It must be made clear that the object is to encourage, not cartels or monopolies, but security of equal opportunity. The advantage which Ford has over Morris or Fiat is not monopoly (he has the fiercest competition with other American manufacturers), but an assurance that, over a large market and not a small one, he will not be subject to a tariff handicap.

As a starting-point and basis for the proposed League support of an exception to the full unconditional M.F.N. clause, the formula of the Economic Committee quoted above might be taken, viz. a reservation "can only be justified in the case of plurilateral conventions of a general character and aiming at the improvement of economic relations between peoples."

As a preliminary step, all negotiating States might begin with an undertaking not to make any increases in their tariffs (absolutely as regards the negotiating States, and also as regards other States unless these States themselves make such increases as in the opinion of an impartial authority to create a new situation justifying a departure from the general rule) for a period sufficient to complete the negotiations, say, three years.

Negotiations for reduction within the association might be based on the following principles:—

No increases in any existing duties of the contracting States;

Classification of present tariff systems (subject to the principles suggested below), into, say, three categories: high, medium, low;

Reduction in general level of all these systems, but a greater reduction in the higher than the medium, and in the medium than in the low.

The normal method to be fixed percentage reductions (high, medium, low) for stated periods.

These percentages to be increased progressively with a view to so reducing the tariffs ultimately that complete abolition would be easy.

(It is possible that the first "ideal" should be equality of all tariffs within the association, not abolition. Such an ideal would involve half the difficulties of a Zollverein, i.e. the determination of the tariffs, but not the other half, viz. distribution.)

The percentage reduction method should, however, not be employed alone. It should be combined with an analysis of the tariffs with a view to the elimination, in whole or in part, from the operation of the automatic reduction of *fiscal* duties, with little or no protective effect (i.e. duties on articles not produced in the country or those which have a corresponding excise), and the complete abolition of duties which are most clearly injurious to the general economy of the countries now imposing them (i.e. duties on industries based on no material resources or experience or special advantages within the country), and of dead and useless duties which discourage consumption rather than encourage production.

The scheme might also provide for the provisional exemption from the percentage system of reduction of very low tariff systems till the level of others has been substantially reduced, and of specially low duties on particular categories of articles which may be found in tariff systems whose general level is not exceptionally low.

Further, the scheme might provide for the most complete and unrestricted application of the M.F.N. clause as between the States in the association, based upon the standard nomenclature and classification now being worked out.

The association should always be open on equal terms to all countries of all continents to join if and when they wish.

Countries not entering the association to be treated equitably.

This to be understood as involving the following principles:—

Countries recognized as having a general level of tariff lower than that of the lowest group within the association to be given the advantage of unconditional M.F.N., though not in the association and though not obliged to have a higher tariff against those outside than inside.

Tariffs not to be raised above the existing—or some new agreed standard not on the whole higher than the present—as against the countries outside the association, subject to the condition defined above.

It is necessary to mention in addition that two other questions of principle of importance are likely to be raised and pressed strongly by certain countries, e.g. Italy, viz. the freedom of movement of men as a corollary to freedom of goods, and the extension of any obligation assumed by the contracting States to their colonies. In the latter connection it must be observed that the distinction between dependent colonies and self-governing Dominions is not so familiar to other countries as it is to Great Britain, and that even within the British Empire there are intermediate systems. The question of freedom of movement of capital may also be raised.

This enumeration of possible conditions of League support for an association involving differential tariffs will at least have served the purpose of showing the intricacy of the whole problem, suggesting as it does the difficulty in securing the conditions, and the dangers which would result from their omission.

There is one other general consideration that should be mentioned. It is obvious that, even if the conditions suggested were secured, the reaction of a country outside, particularly the United States of America, might be simply direct and unqualified resentment against the first practical effect upon itself, i.e. a higher tariff than that applied within the association. This might be such as to prevent any attempt at sympathetic understanding of the other wider objects of the proposals. Retaliation and political friction of the most serious kind might result. It is obvious therefore that elaborate and very careful preparation and presentation are essential.

But with this it would perhaps be not impossible to obtain a sympathetic acceptance of a proposal designed to secure what at the maximum would be the creation of an economic unit equal to that already achieved by the United States of America. For the maximum possible inclusion of countries in an association would not be likely to give a market with larger consuming capacity than that of the United States of America. (The actual spending capacity of the 400 millions of Europe is probably not greater than that of the 120 millions of the United States of America.)

The difficulties then are great and obvious enough. But the alternatives to action on these lines are at least equally discouraging, and the impetus towards action is great and increasing.

It is in these conditions that the decision must be taken as to whether action is to be attempted.

There is this at least to be said in its favour. The actual process of negotiation, if such a procedure involving the direct association of the appropriate Ministers is adopted, would give an education in the principal factors of world commercial policy more effective upon the actual authorities who control action than anything which the League is now doing.

It becomes more and more doubtful whether action

within restricted limits and through our existing committees alone can secure great results, and more and more certain that a more direct association—over a long period of prior preparation—of responsible Ministers is essential if we are to hope for a real transformation of the present position. And if it is true that a large measure of economic *rapprochement* can only come as counterpart of political *rapprochement*, that is no reason for waiting before making a beginning. Each can obviously help the other, and an advance on either line would mean advance on both.

CHAPTER VII

THE FRENCH MEMORANDUM
ON A EUROPEAN FEDERAL UNION

Editor's Foreword

ON May 17, 1930, the Young Plan, which changed the position as regards Reparations, came into operation: the French troops began to evacuate the second and third zones of occupied German territory in the Rhineland: and M. Briand circulated his Memorandum on European Federal Union to the Governments of the European States Members of the League. The following paper was written immediately after receipt of this Memorandum.

The paper was given privately to members of the Secretariat and to such officials of the Governments concerned as desired to have it. Its existence became known to the Press and it was alluded to in certain French and English newspapers as "the 27th Reply" to M. Briand's Memorandum. Its influence was thought to be traceable both in the British reply and in a number of the others. So far as this may have been true, it is of course an instance, not of an international official securing a modification of international policy in accordance with the views of his national Government, but of precisely the opposite.

One of the copies so distributed did in fact reach the hands of one section of the Press, and a substantial part of it was thus published. Otherwise the paper is now printed for the first time.

THE FRENCH MEMORANDUM
ON A EUROPEAN FEDERAL UNION

MAY 20, 1930

BRIEF ANALYSIS

The leading ideas of the [Briand] Memorandum
may be briefly summarized as follows:—

Something in the nature of a "federative organization" of Europe is needed in the interests alike of
the peace and of the economic and social well-being of
the continent.

This organization must, however, be such as to
respect both national sovereignties and the overriding
authority of the League.

With this object European Governments are asked
to give their opinions on four proposals:—

1. The conclusion of a General Pact, engaging the
Governments to take part in periodic or special meetings to ensure regular contact on all questions of special
interest to Europe.

2. The establishment of the following special organs:—

An annual Conference consisting of the European
members of the League, under a President
changing at each meeting.

An executive Committee, consisting of a limited
number of these members, meeting at Geneva at
the same periods as the Council, under a President
similarly changing.

A separate Secretariat if and when required, though the partial and temporary utilization of the League is not excluded.

3. The establishment of certain fundamental principles which are suggested as,

The general subordination of the economic to the political problem.

The conception of European political co-operation. Economic *rapprochement* in Europe, under political responsibility, as the essential purpose of European economic policy.

4. Programme of co-operation; of methods of study; of collaboration with outside countries.

The subjects mentioned cover Economies, Transit, Finance, Labour, Health, and Intellectual Co-operation.

The Memorandum asks for replies by July 15th with a view to decisions by a European Conference to be held at Geneva next September.

GENERAL COMMENTS

While the fundamental conception is political, the programme of work is predominantly economic (in the wide sense including labour, transit, and finance questions). In the two other subjects mentioned—health and intellectual co-operation—the problems tend to be either more local or more universal: few are likely to be European.

In economic problems recent experience certainly gives strong confirmation of some of the leading ideas of the Memorandum.

We have seen that existing economic policies are

so strongly buttressed by vested interests in the different countries that there is little hope of securing substantial change unless economic are reinforced by political motives—and Ministers of Commerce are supported, and influenced, by the Foreign Ministers, who in turn are determined to realize an ideal of greater solidarity. If, therefore, the proposed association of political and economical authorities means that existing European security justifies, and greater European security should be largely attained by, closer economic co-operation and the removal of present barriers (and not that closer economic co-operation must first wait for greater security), it offers a most powerful, and indeed indispensable, assistance to the League's economic work.

At the same time the economic reasons are constantly becoming stronger. It is not so much that trade barriers are higher or more numerous (though they are) as that the technical developments of industry constantly increase the advantage of large-scale production (and therefore of secure access to large markets). Moreover, apart from the actual waste involved in the present small units, the dangers resulting from the great disparity between the great unit of the United States and the small ones of Europe become more evident. And this, the central international problem in the economic sphere, is overwhelmingly a European question. There is nothing elsewhere comparable to the combination in Europe of advanced industrial development and small tariff units.

This has received a most impressive demonstration in the last Assembly's programme of action and its sequel. A Conference was convened in order to arrest the increase of tariffs for a time, and in that time to negotiate closer co-operation. All countries were invited, but by a process of self-selection the Conference became European, for all European countries except Russia and Albania sent delegates, while only four non-European countries did so. What followed is even more striking. A Commercial Convention providing, within limits, a certain temporary stabilization was combined with a Programme of Negotiations. The signatories of one or both include practically all Europe (twenty-three countries already) and *no* country outside Europe. The range of subjects includes almost all the most important economic problems on which the League is working, and corresponds closely with those included in the French Memorandum. The subsequent negotiations are entirely in the hands of the signatory, i.e. European, States; for only those States participate unless they agree to invite others.

At the same time this essentially European work is in a real sense "within the framework of the League." For it has developed in accordance with a programme approved by the full Assembly; the European composition of the series of conferences has resulted from a process of self-selection; the Assembly and Council will be informed of progress, and will control procedure both by decisions as to convocation, and by budget provision; the organs of the League, including both Secretariat and technical Committees, and those only, will be utilized; and lastly, the results of the limited negotiations are to be reviewed by a "universal" conference.

We have therefore already started on a "European" task closely similar to that proposed in the Memorandum, and are committed to finding appropriate methods and machinery within the League organization. This task is almost identical with that of the Memorandum as regards economic questions with which as explained above it is predominantly concerned.

This task already commenced should therefore, unless it is interrupted or replaced by an external and alternative procedure, give most of what the Memorandum requires; and it has developed, or must develop, the appropriate machinery, within the limits of existing organization and existing decisions—with one important exception. The economic negotiations are under the control of economic officials and Ministers of Commerce; the present arrangements do not effectively subject them to political control or relate them to general political ideals or policy. This, however, would be a simple addition to make. If the Council appointed a "European" Committee of the Council, to follow and control these European negotiations, consisting of the European members of the Council (possibly with some additions) and reporting to the full Council as the Austrian, Hungarian, and Greek Committees do—we should have not only a European programme, but also a corresponding machinery, all *really* within the framework of the League.

Important questions of principle are indeed raised to which we will return later. But it will be convenient first to examine the Memorandum's proposals as to organization.

ORGANIZATION

The French Government intends to keep within the framework of the League, and to avoid either diminishing the League's authority or impeding its work.

The actual proposals seem inconsistent with these intentions.

An annual Conference is to be held at Geneva during September, and is presumably to consist of the European Delegates (or some of them) to the Assembly.

Similarly, a Permanent Executive Committee is to meet at Geneva at the same periods as the Council, presumably also consisting of the European members of the Council.

But neither Conference nor Committee will derive its authority in any way from the Covenant, or be in any way controlled by the prescriptions, or subject to the rules and safeguards, of the Covenant; they will be self-constituted, and so far as they relate their work, in its universal aspects, to the policies and interests of other countries, it will be by virtue of spontaneous and specific decisions and not of any rights enjoyed, or of a machinery partly controlled, by those other States.

As to whether the external and parallel organization should be carried further and include also a separate Secretariat and separate technical committees, the Memorandum is hesitating. It contemplates the possibility of both, but does not pronounce decisively. This is a crucial part of the organization proposals, and we must therefore consider what would follow logically from the main principle of an external European Conference and Executive Committee.

The reason for proposing an organization on this principle, instead of the constitution of European Committees within, and subject to, the League organs, is obvious. It is desired to deal with specifically European problems, or European aspects of universal problems,—to base agreements upon specifically European interests. How can a "universal" League budget fairly bear the cost; but above all how can such negotiations be subjected to the control of an authority in which other countries exercise a partial control, and may, where unanimity is required, impose a veto?

But an organization based on this consideration can clearly not stop short at a Conference and a Committee, and rely upon the League Secretariat and technical committees for the rest. If the very purpose of making the supreme authorities for this work independent of the League is that they may be free to proceed with negotiations of a kind which would be vetoed by the League authorities, how is it possible that the League Secretariat and League technical committees, both supported by the general League budget, should be utilized to prepare and secure practical effect to such negotiations? How can the League call conferences to secure conventions to embody a policy which *ex hypothesi* could not be developed if subject to the supreme control of the League Council and Assembly?

A European Conference and Committee must therefore have their work prepared by their own permanent officials and their own expert committees; and must call their own conferences and negotiate their own conventions. The organization must be parallel and fully equipped throughout. And as the problems are the same in character as those dealt with by something like half the League organization, the mechanism would require, if the work is to be adequately prepared, to be more or less as large and as expensive as the relevant technical sections of the League Secretariat and Labour Office.

We must therefore apparently imagine a European Assembly, a European Council, a European Economic Committee, Financial Committee, Transit Commission (to say nothing of Labour, Health, and Intellectual Co-operation questions), and a host of more specialized sub-committees meeting at Geneva, and consisting presumably of the same persons who are the European members of the corresponding League bodies, and studying the same problems as the League. But they would all be, both formally and really, outside the League; for they would not be subject in any way to the control of the League authorities; would be served by a separate Secretariat; and have their expenses met from other sources than the League budget.

Such an organization, if additional to the League's, would obviously be impracticably expensive; would involve an impossible problem of co-ordination; and would certainly prevent the effective execution of the League's work on the same problems on universal lines.

For the difficulty is in one respect even greater than has been stated above. In the nature of the case, for each of the particular problems to be dealt with ("prohibitions," treatment of foreigners, tariff agreements, veterinary regulations, etc.), the time at which they are ripe for a purely European treatment, if that is to be arranged, is somewhat earlier than that at which more universal agreements can be reached. The pioneer work would be done by the European organization. The logical consequence would be to transfer the best and the bulk of the League personnel, and devote most of the meetings of the expert committees, to the new external European organization, leaving the League with the mere shell, with a largely reduced mechanism, following behind and from time to time trying to universalize an agreement already concluded within Europe by an external organization.

This is obviously not the intention. But nothing short of this really escapes, on this principle, the difficulty of the "regional problem."

We are therefore forced to consider whether we cannot solve the problem of dealing with regional questions fully within the framework of the League,— so fully that the League mechanism can itself be used without any parallel and external institution.

I think we can, and must. But the fundamental principles of League development are involved in this question.

REGIONALIZING WITHIN THE LEAGUE

The primary task of the League, the prevention of war, is in its nature "universal," since the causes of war, its range if it breaks out, its effects, and the sanctions required to stop it, all tend to be world wide. For duties directly related to this primary task, League members would certainly desire, as the Memorandum

does, that the League's authority should be permanent
and decisive.

But as we get further from the last war, and conditions become more stable, the bulk of international
questions are in the nature of co-operative agreements
and negotiations not closely and immediately connected with threats of war; and a large proportion
of these are in many vital respects, though not all,
local or regional in character. We reconstruct Hungary; or we embark on economic negotiations of which
a first step must sometimes be European, or regional
within Europe, the more universal agreement being
slighter and perhaps later. More and more work of
this kind may have to start with regional arrangements
built up into something wider by extension or co-
ordination.

Is this work to be done outside the League or inside?
In some cases, indeed, it is a matter of minor expediency. Many minor arrangements between contiguous
countries may, without serious results, be carried
through simply and directly by those countries themselves. It is enough that they should be within the
League framework in the restricted sense in which the
Memorandum uses the term, i.e. that they should not
conflict with League principles. But when the area
of such external arrangements is as wide as Europe,
a fifth of the world's population and at least four-fifths
of the League's strength, when the mechanism employed is permanent and parallel, when the subjects
dealt with include a large proportion of the League's
"co-operation" tasks, the results must be extremely
serious.

In the first place, a powerful impulse is given to the organization of the world into a few large groups —Europe, Pan-American, British Empire (with perhaps a Russian and an Asiatic to follow)—each equipped with an organization absorbing the bulk of the work on practical and current problems.

True, "universal" work would remain: the study of general questions which have no specifically European aspect might be continued; co-ordination between the results of the different groups would be needed; and ultimately "universal" questions of peace and war would arise. But it is very doubtful whether the League —its organization, its traditions, its authority based on prestige and public confidence—if divorced from the bulk of current and daily business, would retain strength for the time of need. The more the developing organization of the world becomes regional, the wider and richer the regions, the less chance will the universal organ have of making universal interests and principles ultimately prevail. A strong impetus would be given to the development of both the economic and political life of the world in large regional units. Movements and problems which might have been, and should have been, universal, will become regional. Unnecessary regional and local difficulties will be created. There will be a conflict between the regional and the central in which the latter would constantly tend to be weaker. More and more the League would tend, both in economic problems and in questions involving dangers of war to come in at a later, and too late, stage. We should have, more remotely, but ultimately on a larger scale, the same kind of danger which comes from "alliances" endangering the League's overriding authority. If the League's influence is not a factor in the developing life of the world out of which the forces making for peace and war grow, it will certainly be impotent to stop the consequences.

To make this point more concrete:—a European consideration of economic problems must involve some real or apparent conflict of interests with other countries. Some form of differential tariff is the most obvious example, but the same difficulties will arise in other forms. It is surely of the utmost importance that any such European policy should be so developed and negotiated as not to be regarded as a hostile conspiracy by other countries. If this is possible, it is possible within the full League framework and along such a procedure as laid down by the last Assembly. If it cannot be, and if acceptance is only possible by means of conferences restricted at every stage to European Powers, the danger to future peace is obviously very great. The League would probably not hold back the forces that would be ultimately engendered. The League procedure and mechanism, developed on the lines laid down last September, can explore and exploit every possibility of acceptance, while still retaining a power of restraint and a safeguard for proposals that go beyond that possibility.

The development of the principle of the Assembly resolution of last September, in such a way as to be compatible with the purposes alike of the Convention of March (see p. 109) and the French Memorandum, means, I suggest, something like the following arrangement.

Meetings of the signatories (European) of the March Convention (with other countries when they decided to invite them) would take place as arranged, under League convocation and arrangements made by the League Secretariat, and paid for (as far as Secretariat services are concerned) from the League budget.

Similarly, the League committees should, meeting as such, prepare the work and should arrange, as they find convenient, for sub-committees consisting of European members only.

Reports would, as on all other work, come before the Council and Assembly, who would exercise the normal control, through comment, convocation, and budget provision.

The results would (as provided in the Assembly resolution) be examined in due course by a "universal" conference.

Meantime (in order to secure the desired "political" control), the whole of the work could be controlled by a European Committee of the Council.

This Committee might work (like the Hungarian Committee) with the association of European countries not members of the Council; but would report to the full Council.

Similarly, with the same object, a Conference of European States might meet each September. But again, it should report to the full Assembly.

Such an organization would be in accordance with precedents and existing decisions, and would justify the full use of the League machinery and avoid the creation of a parallel organization. At the same time, it would be practical and workable, and would involve no difficulty, except in the case of proposals for which other countries insisted on imposing a veto.

Is this exception so fatal as to make action within the League impossible? Here is the crux of the question. Let us see just what it means.

The separate examination within the League of regional or European problems, and European agreements embodying policy which other countries do not accept for themselves, but which they do not strongly object to European countries adopting *inter se*, are both certainly practicable within the League machinery. So much is clear from the Assembly resolution of September and the March Convention. There remains the possibility that European countries would wish to negotiate an agreement *inter se* which they could not persuade other countries to regard as anything but injurious or hostile to themselves. Doubtless the League machinery would impede the conclusion of such agreements. But is not this desirable on every ground? Is it not of the utmost importance that every possible effort should be made so to negotiate and so to explain European agreements to the rest of the world that the world will accept them as *not* hostile? Negotiation within the League would secure this automatically. Negotiation outside from the first would make it much less likely. In the last resort, European countries could always break away and make their own negotiations. But surely this should be only the last resort, not the first step; and in any case the conclusion of agreements, and the establishment of the economic policy and development of Europe, on a basis which other countries could not be persuaded to accept as anything but injurious to themselves, would be a most serious thing, fraught with incalculable dangers of every kind.

"Regionalizing," therefore, so far as it is desirable, should, I suggest, be within the League, not outside it.

Some consequences are, indeed, involved. The League must be prepared, and must do its utmost to meet, similar regional needs in other parts of the world. To the extent to which such needs develop and are dealt with, the League at once remains a balanced whole and controls the real developing life of the world. To the extent, however, to which such non-European work lags behind, a budget problem certainly arises. Either the extra work done for Europe must be taken as a factor in assessing allocation or an estimate of the extra work for Europe must be made and a supplementary toll taken from European countries. The former is undesirable because it would give an inducement to every country to show how little the League did for it, and because the allocation ratios would require frequent change. The latter would be simple, for either a simple percentage addition could be agreed upon or an agreed total sum could be automatically partitioned among European countries on the standard allocation ratios.

BRITISH ATTITUDE

Great Britain will have a difficult decision as to her relation to any European policies that may be ultimately evolved. But I think it is of great importance that she should be associated at least for the earlier stages, for the following reasons.

(*a*) By joining, she will exercise her influence in securing that the development both of organization and of policy is compatible with the essentials of her "universal" interests. Great Britain is the indispensable intermediary between the European and the world point of view. If she stands out, either the European organization will collapse and a movement which has possibilities of great benefit be thrown away or it will succeed, in which case the dangerous elements will be less restrained, and Great Britain pushed irrevocably into the "transatlantic and imperial" sphere of thought and policy—the one fatal impediment to a universal system.

(*b*) From inside she will be in a strong position to make her influence effective, without losing her right of dissociation under such conditions, or to such extent, as may ultimately prove desirable.

In other words, she loses nothing, and may gain much, by taking part effectively in the early stages of the development.

***

CONCLUDING NOTE

The greater part of the above note has necessarily been devoted to examining one important principle of the proposed organization. It is hoped that this will not be interpreted as any criticism of the main conception of a more united Europe. It is, indeed, obvious that, for economic as well as political reasons, a greater solidarity between the countries of Europe is of the utmost possible importance. The inescapable interdependence is demonstrated by all that we attempt;

too often negatively, in the form that a convention desired by nearly all countries cannot be applied if a single important country stands out. It is an urgent necessity that this interdependence shall find its expression (through the development of the main conception and policy of the Memorandum) in a positive force helping co-operation, instead of in a negative force impeding it. The Pact of solidarity proposed in Point 1 may well be the basis of a new constructive effort which will at last enable the obstacles which have obstructed progress during recent years to be surmounted.

POSTSCRIPT

ALL the twenty-six Governments which replied to the French Memorandum expressed full agreement with the ideal of closer European co-operation: but few agreed as to the form and method of this co-operation.

All the States, except Holland, agreed that this European association should be "on the plane of absolute sovereignty and of entire political independence."

Most of the States were prepared to join in a system of conference provided that there were no elaborate organization or rigid form of union, and provided, especially, that there were no danger to the efficiency and authority of the League. But hardly any supported the idea of creating a new permanent political committee or a new Secretariat.

As regards membership, some States advocated inclusion of European States not Members of the League, viz. the Soviet Union and Turkey. Most of the Governments disagreed with the French view that the economic problem should be subordinated to the political. Germany, replying to M. Briand's argument as to the need for organizing security, took occasion again to press her case for equality of status and for peaceful reform of conditions recognized as untenable; and Italy said that only on the basis of general disarmament could the association be established.

Many of the Governments stressed the danger of intercontinental rivalries, unless the European union were to be completely within the League.

The British reply recognized the desirability of closer co-operation, primarily on the economic side: it held that the establishment of new and independent institutions was unnecessary and undesirable; that the organization proposed would have no authority from the Covenant, no organic connection with the League, and no safeguards; and that there would be danger of creating confusion and rivalries, and of impairing the authority and efficiency of the League. It was essential, from the British standpoint, to avoid inter-continental rivalries. The purpose of the project, it was claimed, could be achieved within the League's framework, by setting up European Committees of the various organs of the League.

The replies, collected in a French White Paper, were considered by a meeting of the European Members of the League on September 8, 1930. The meeting showed little prospect of agreement on any substantial project of European union: and M. Briand made a disheartened speech in the Assembly.[1]

But the project was not dead. The outcome was a scheme under which a European Commission was established, under conditions defining its relationship to the policy of the League Council and Assembly so as to provide safeguards against the danger that had been apprehended. This Commission has since been working (in so far as it has been used) as part of the League's machinery, served by the League Secretariat, and having as its Secretary the League's Secretary-General.   ED.

[1] For a Summary of the French Memorandum and the twenty-six replies, see *Bulletin of International News*, Royal Institute of International Affairs, September 11, 1930.

CHAPTER VIII

THE INTERNATIONAL CHARACTER OF THE LEAGUE SECRETARIAT

Editor's Foreword

THIS paper was written when the question of the better organization of the Secretariat, and of maintaining unimpaired its international character, had lately been raised in the Tenth Assembly.

In the early days of the League, Lord Balfour, in a Report to the Council, had emphasized that "nothing should be allowed to weaken, in the minds of the staff of the League, the feeling that it is engaged in an international and not a national cause." And this principle is laid down in the first article of the League's Staff Regulations.

Now, at the beginning of 1930, when the League had been officially in existence for just ten years, a Special Committee of enquiry had just been formed, "to examine what steps could be taken to ensure in the future as in the past the best possible administrative results for the Secretariat, the I.L.O., and the Registry of the Permanent Court of International Justice." Three principles had been laid down by the Assembly. That the staff should as far as possible have permanent employment and contracts of long duration. (This had a bearing upon the international character of the Secretariat, for an international civil servant who could look forward to no tolerably assured prospect of a career in the international service would inevitably tend to look more anxiously after his prospects of national service at home.) That throughout the whole Secretariat and I.L.O. every post should be open to be filled by promotion from among the whole body of officials.

That the system of selection, and recruitment of the staff, while taking full account of an equitable distribution of posts among the different nationalities, should be particularly stringent in order to ensure that the officials who become members of the permanent international civil service should have the character, abilities, and training required.

Lastly, provision should be made for adequate pensions.

The discussions about this, in 1929, 1930, and 1931, showed that some Governments, notably those of Italy and Germany, desired that the higher officials should be present rather as agents of national policies within the Secretariat than as international civil servants.

(For the outcome, see Postscript.)

THE INTERNATIONAL CHARACTER OF
THE LEAGUE SECRETARIAT

JANUARY 13, 1930

THE crucial problem of the constitution of the Secretariat is to secure and maintain its international character.

This problem is one for which no analogy exists in national administrations; and it is not to be solved on lines which aim at the elimination of all consciousness of nationality or special knowledge of national conditions in the personnel. No analogy, for example, is to be found in the incorporation in one British service of English, Scots, and Welsh, with the expectation that in the course of their work they will be unconscious of their different national origins. The question is much more complex than that, and to face it we must start with some of the fundamental characteristics of the League.

The first of these is that the League is neither a super-State, nor a single unitary State, nor a mere collection of separate States. Its policy is not formed by the mere addition of the policies of the different States; nor even by a mere process of compromise and concession between these different policies. It is of the essence of the League that this process takes place under the influence of the guiding principles of the Covenant; under the influence of the traditions of the League in

action; and under the influence of those States who
on any given issue are "disinterested," i.e. interested
not as separate States in the exact effect of the particular decision, but interested only that the decision
should be arrived at by methods, and be itself of a
character, consistent with the League's principles and
traditions. The influence of such States (Sweden in
the past has often been a notable example) has been
a vital and indispensable element in the amalgam of
forces out of which the decision emerges. In League
decisions, a "corporate League sense" (the sense that
the League is more than the sum of its component
parts) in the League authorities—especially the Council
—is vital; and in the development and maintenance
of this corporate sense the positive influence of disinterested States is indispensable.

But the Council changes in personnel and meets only
three times a year. Some other and more continuous
depositary of the corporate League sense is needed;
and it is the feeling of this need which inspires those
who attach such an importance to the international
character of the Secretariat.

Those who are acquainted with the actual working
of the League, with the discontinuous meetings of its
supreme authorities, with the intricacy of the preparations which precede and so largely determine the
decisions of those authorities, will know that this rôle
cannot be successfully sustained by the Secretariat
unless it contains within it a real, intimate, and
live knowledge of the conditions, varying forces and

factors, and developing policies, of the different countries.

A Secretariat composed wholly of persons separated, except for occasional periods of leave, from all contact with their countries, and all receiving the same undifferentiated formation of mental outlook and sympathy throughout all their working lives, would doubtless be international in character; but it would be inadequate for much of its work and ineffective in its influence.

This is half the truth. The other half is at least equally important and the main basis of the Assembly's preoccupation. If an undue proportion of the members of the Secretariat look to their national Governments for their permanent career, in which their League appointment is only an interlude; if, in particular, this applies to most or all of the highest League appointments; then it will be difficult to create and maintain a Secretariat tradition which will effectively prevent individual members from considering it among their rights and duties to try to facilitate the adoption of their own country's policy. Such a breaking-up of the Secretariat, and abuse of its functions, would of course be even more disastrous than the weakness of a permanently expatriated and denationalized body.

This aspect of the problem is, however, so fully realized by those for whom this paper is intended that I need not further elaborate it. I return therefore to the other aspect.

I believe myself that, among the forces required to maintain a real League corporate sense, the influence of an international Secretariat is absolutely essential; that this means that it should be among the actual and practical functions of the Secretariat to prepare the conditions for future decisions and agreement; and that for this it is indispensable that, among members of the Secretariat, there should be those who remain in intimate contact with their respective countries and can thus bring special knowledge to the work of preparation.

A clearer conception of this kind of function, and a clear definition of its conditions and its limits, is imperatively necessary. I would myself define it as follows:—

A member of the Secretariat should in no sense whatever be an Ambassador for his country; he should in no case advocate or try to secure the adoption of a policy because it is the policy of the Government of his country. But it is right, and in some cases indispensable, that he should actively desire and work for *a* solution, and a solution which is both possible, having regard to the known policies of the different countries concerned, and of a kind compatible with the general aims and spirit of the League; and that in Secretariat preparations he should bring some special knowledge, not possessed by his colleagues of other nationalities, of the main factors in the policy of his country, e.g. as to where that policy is likely to be elastic, and where rigid, in what directions concession is most possible or least possible. It is right, and sometimes of great value, that such knowledge should be pooled between Secretariat members of different nationalities, and that this pooled knowledge should be available in the Secretariat's preparations. And as a part of these arrangements it is often right, and desirable, that Secretariat members should be in touch with their respective national delegations, and should help future agreement by discussions as to probable reactions of other countries.

If the Secretariat is to take any part of value in maintaining the League corporate sense, there *must* be among its members those who fulfil such functions, and these functions must be regarded as legitimate. Of course this does not apply in equal measure to all members and all ranks and offices in the Secretariat. A considerable number need have, and should have, no such functions. Others, who can usefully bring special national knowledge, need only do so as to objective facts little involved with policies (e.g. those in the Economic Intelligence Section). But a number of the senior officers *must* do more than this.

In fact, of course, they do. But the fact that they do so on the basis of no clearly defined and understood conception of the limits of an international officer's rights and duties, results sometimes in their work, often their best work, assuming the appearance of being regarded as "intrigue," sometimes in its passing the true line and becoming national advocacy.

The difficulties and dangers of these functions are of course obvious. There must obviously be limits to such a process. It can only be one element in the preparations. It cannot be a substitute for direct contact between national delegations. No rule distinguishing between the legitimate action, and that which crosses the line and becomes national advocacy, is capable of automatic application. It is only too easy to make such criticisms and to arrive at the easy solution of excluding all such functions as illegitimate, with corresponding conclusions as to the constitution of the personnel.

But it remains true that there is a real distinction between working for a League solution and bringing elements of special national knowledge to the task on the one hand, and advocating national policy on the other. It is a distinction which a loyal League servant can understand in and through his actual work; he can make it the rule of his personal conduct, and can see which of his colleagues do and do not understand and apply it.

All who know the League's work will realize that, before meetings of the Council, and other meetings of governmental representatives, at Geneva, much preparation is required. Contacts of the delegates, and of the national delegations at Geneva, are not enough. Nor is it enough to supplement this by correspondence between the Governments or by means of the Legation machinery of the diplomatic services. All this is needed, but it is not enough. Preparation, involving some knowledge of differing national points of view, between sessions and at Geneva, is essential.

There is therefore only one alternative to the exercise by the Secretariat of functions I have tried to describe. This is, that the different countries—including in particular the principal ones, the permanent Member States on the Council—should have *resident representatives* at Geneva. With this system, it may be said, the ambiguous, border-line, functions of the Secretariat can be suppressed, and the consequential question about recruitment of personnel becomes simple.

Is this a practicable and desirable system? I believe not. I believe nothing would be so likely to destroy the essential League spirit. Let us examine it.

This system is in operation as regards distant countries and countries not normally on the Council, whose responsible Ministers are not therefore in direct contact—with their attendant delegations—several times a year. In these cases the system has obvious advantages which perhaps outweigh any objections. But no European Great Power has a resident representative of this kind entrusted with any League duties. The idea has been suggested several times, but always dropped, I think for decisive reasons. Let us see how it would work.

If any European Great Power starts the practice, it is likely to be followed by the others. Even if the first person appointed is of relatively junior rank—say, Counsellor of Embassy—some other great country will go one better and appoint a Minister. The whole will then be levelled up to Ministerial, and perhaps in time, Ambassadorial, rank. There will be staff and experts, and we shall have a series of Legations in Geneva. These Legations will follow all League work, and inevitably Council meetings will be preceded by "shadow councils" of the Ministers of the countries in the Council. Each of these Ministers will derive his instructions from his Foreign Office—and in actual working normally from the Office rather than the Foreign Minister. By these means the work will be so fully prepared that the Council members will find their task limited to ratification of agreements already reached or the decision of a few outstanding points of special difficulty. All this is very attractive—much too attractive—for it will inevitably have the following results :—

(*a*) The system will approximate to that of the Conference of Ambassadors, in personnel, in tradition, in outlook, in the source of authority.

(*b*) Foreign Ministers, under the pressure of their work at home, will discover to an increasing extent that their resident Ministers can represent them, and that it is not worth their while to attend. The Council will lose its distinctive character—everything that distinguishes it from an enlarged Conference of Ambassadors.

(*c*) It will also be more difficult to secure the presence of specialists at conferences.

(*d*) In face of a permanent corps of Ministers, meeting in committees and "shadow councils" and in direct contact with their Foreign Office, the Secretariat will necessarily sink in status, in influence, and in the character of its personnel, to clerks responsible only for routine duties. They will cease to be an element of importance in the formation or maintenance of the League's traditions.

(*e*) These traditions will thus depend upon the resident Ministers. These will be essentially and exclusively *national*—and will represent those national elements which are developed and expressed through the national Foreign Offices. And experience shows that residence abroad, under such conditions, tends, not to mitigate, but to exaggerate the national outlook. The national Delegations on the Reparation Commission were always more national and intransigeant than their instructing Ministers—and the whole history of reparation is that of attempts to escape the deadlock so created by the double method of conferences of Ministers and the calling in of experts, i.e. by a reversion to the League system.

I have seen this system worked out, and worked through, at the Reparation Commission[1]—its effect on the spirit of the national delegates and upon the function of the international Secretariat. I am certain that such a system will be fatally destructive of precisely those distinctive elements which the League has in its early years brought into international negotiations.

What is the alternative? I can see none except a *double system*, which includes within the Secretariat, and within all the higher ranks, both those for whom the League is a life career and those who have recently come from, and perhaps may soon again return to, their respective countries. The first might

[1] The author was Secretary-General to the Reparation Commission from 1920 to July 1923.—ED.

be recruited young, given the same kind of life-tenure
as national civil servants, and like them assured of
retiring pensions; the second might come and go more
or less on a short-term basis, though subject to some
precautions not now applied. There might be a standard proportion—though not necessarily an absolutely
unvarying proportion—for each rank. It goes without
saying that the first category, who have life-appoint-
ments, should sever all connection with national
services, and should give assurances that they do not
contemplate ever returning to national public service.
I do not propose to work out the details, but only
to emphasize the main principles, in the present note.

This may seem a complicated, unprecedented system; and the international officer imagined, a queer
hermaphroditic creature.

But the problem, too, is complex and without precedent; and the new international officer needed for
the League's task *is* something new in the world's
history.

We can't cut the Gordian knot—a simple solution
is just a plain evasion of the real problem—which is
one of immense intricacy and inestimable importance.

POSTSCRIPT

THE Committee of Thirteen on Organization of the Secretariat, which had been set up by the Tenth Assembly, failed to reach agreement, chiefly on account of the insistence of Italy and Germany on the national principle in the higher appointments.

At the Eleventh Assembly, decisions were reached after long discussion, Italy and Germany being in a small minority; the international principle was reaffirmed; the first article of the Staff Regulations was strengthened, not weakened; it was proposed that thereafter every new official should sign an undertaking emphasizing the international character of the League's service.

A decision in favour of long term contracts for Secretariat appointments was also reached by a majority vote. But on the question of adding to the number of Under-Secretaries there was inconclusive debate.

This matter came up again in 1932, at the Thirteenth Assembly. The Secretary-General, Sir Eric Drummond, was about to retire, and also two of the Under-Secretaries-General, or possibly all three.

The proposal was made by Spain that the posts of Under-Secretary-General should be suppressed. This led to a keen discussion on the maintenance of the international character of the Secretariat. The Italian delegate again emphasized the national principle: the Norwegian delegate, on the contrary, stressed the importance of the opportunity, when all the higher posts were falling vacant, to make a move away from the system of representation of Great Powers "in the direction of democracy."

Later, it was resolved that the posts of Under-Secretary-General should be retained, but that there should be two Deputy Secretaries-General instead of one. The intention of the change was to "make it possible to assign one of these posts to a national of a Member not permanently represented on the Council, in the event of the Secretary-

General having been chosen from among the nationals of Members permanently represented on the Council."

It is evident from this text, passed by the Thirteenth Assembly, that the idea of earmarking the higher posts for nationals of particular States was now being more firmly entrenched than before.

The Assembly also agreed to a "declaration of loyalty," to be made by officials of the Secretariat and International Labour Office as follows :—

> "I solemnly undertake in all loyalty, discretion, and conscience the functions that have been entrusted to me as (Secretary-General) of the League of Nations to discharge my functions and to regulate my conduct with the interests of the League alone in view and not to seek or receive instructions from any Government or other authority external."   ED.

PART II

THE WEAPONS OF THE LEAGUE

INTRODUCTION TO PART II

The papers collected in this part of the book deal almost entirely with one of the most controversial of all subjects concerning the League—the question of the League's powers for preventing and stopping war.

What will still appear to many people the initial question—whether the League ought to have any such powers at all—is left out of consideration in these papers: for that question lies outside the framework within which the author was working—viz. the League's Covenant. That Covenant provides for certain economic and other sanctions; and what he was here concerned with was the question—how they should be elaborated and applied, especially for the purpose of *preventing* war. The series of papers, written at intervals between 1919 and 1929, shows how the question presented itself from time to time to an international civil servant, and how his answer to it developed and was adjusted to the changing circumstances.

The circumstances did change very much: during the years since the Covenant was framed, there have been wide fluctuations in the amount of support given by public opinion, and by the Governments chiefly concerned, to the whole principle of sanctions and of "collective security" against war. An attempt has been made, in the Forewords and Postscripts to the papers, to indicate the circumstances in which each was written and the subsequent developments.　　Ed.

CHAPTER IX

THE ECONOMIC WEAPONS OF THE LEAGUE UNDER ARTICLE XVI OF THE COVENANT

Editor's Foreword

THE following study of the League's powers of coercion under Article XVI of the Covenant was written so early as September 1919. The Covenant had been signed only three months earlier, the nucleus of the Secretariat had not yet been transferred from London to Geneva, the League Council had not yet held its first meeting; indeed, the League was not yet officially in being.

At that time the need for some coercive powers, to repress resort to war in breach of the Covenant, had hardly been challenged. All the national spokesmen, Allied and neutral, who had lately participated in the drafting of the Covenant, had recognized this need,[1] and none had been more emphatic about it than President Wilson: indeed, the President's chief contribution to the Covenant was the guarantee given in Article X, which, as he recognized, led logically to the Sanctions Clauses.[2] As for the British position at that time, it is sufficiently indicated by the fact that the chief article concerning sanctions, Article

---

[1] Except for a brief period, a delegate of Norway.—ED.

[2] Two of President Wilson's predecessors in the Presidency, Roosevelt and Taft, had likewise supported the principle of sanctions; cf. Mr. Roosevelt's speech in 1910 on receiving the Nobel Peace Prize. "Finally, it would be a master stroke if the Powers honestly bent on peace would form a league of peace, not only to keep the peace among themselves but to prevent, by force if necessary, its being broken by others." (Quoted by Morley, *Society of Nations*, p. 6); cf. also the plan of the League of Peace proposed by Mr. Taft, Philadelphia, June 1915 (ibid.).—ED.

XVI, corresponds closely in substance and wording with the draft prepared for the British Government in 1918 by an official committee under Lord Phillimore. Written in these circumstances, the paper is simply a severe study of the means of making the League's powers effective. There was no need then to take account of the absence of the United States from the League system.

It should be noted that the paper deals primarily with the League's economic weapon, and deals only with the League's powers under one Article, Article XVI, which refers exclusively to cases when resort to war in breach of the Covenant has been committed. No attempt is made here to deal with the League's power to exercise pressure under Articles X, XI, or XV for the prevention of war, or its responsibility under Article XIII, paragraph 4, for proposing the steps to be taken to give effect to an arbitral award.

THE ECONOMIC WEAPONS OF THE LEAGUE UNDER ARTICLE XVI OF THE COVENANT

September 1919

REASONS FOR IMMEDIATE CONSIDERATION

It appears desirable for the following reasons that the question of the preparations required to enable the League to use, if necessity arises, the weapon of economic and financial blockade[1] contemplated in Article XVI of the Treaty should be considered by the Council and, on reference from the Council, by the First Assembly of the League.

The use of this weapon is in certain circumstances a specific duty imposed by Article XVI. This duty cannot be effectively carried out without great loss of time and efficiency unless there has been considerable previous preparation before the time at which action is required.

In the present state of the world it appears not improbable that situations will arise in which the use of the weapon will be necessary; or at least the knowledge that the weapon is ready for use may have a very salutary effect.

One of the most serious weaknesses of the League at present is perhaps that so many people think that it is founded more upon good intentions than upon a cool

[1] The word "blockade" is used throughout this paper, not in the strict technical sense of the Declaration of Paris, but in the popular sense in which it was current during the Great War.—ED.

consideration of the stern realities of international trouble. It is therefore desirable on general grounds that, while the first meetings of the Council and of the Assembly should give the world the positive hope of removing misunderstandings and promoting international co-operation, they should also show quite clearly that the Members of the League as a whole are determined, if necessity arises, to enforce their will by effective action on any particular country which, in the circumstances contemplated by the Covenant, defies the general verdict of the world.[1]

THE PROVISIONS OF THE TREATY

The relevant article of the Treaty (XVI) runs as follows :—

> "Should any Member of the League resort to war in disregard of its Covenants under Articles XII, XIII, or XV, it shall *ipso facto* be deemed to have committed an act of war against all other Members of the League, which hereby undertake immediately to subject it to the severance of all trade or financial relations . . . and the prevention of all financial, commercial, or personal intercourse between the nationals of the Covenant-breaking State and the nationals of any other State whether a Member of the League or not.

[1] The wording here is perhaps open to misconstruction. The sanctions of Article XVI are not applicable, as some American critics have supposed, simply as a means of imposing "the general verdict of the world" (as represented by the League Council) upon a recalcitrant State : they apply only against a State Member of the League which "resort(s) to war" in violation of its own treaty pledges.—ED.

K

"It shall be the duty of the Council in such cases to recommend to the several Governments concerned what effective military, naval, or air forces the Members of the League shall severally contribute to the armed forces to be used to protect the Covenants of the League.

"The Members of the League agree, further, that they will mutually support one another in the financial and economic measures which are taken under this article, in order to minimize the loss and inconvenience resulting from the above measures," . . . .

The following conclusions appear to emerge from the above provisions:—

(a) The Treaty does not definitely contemplate the use of the economic weapon unless a Member of the League should "resort to war in disregard of its covenants" under certain specified articles. The case of a country, for instance, in effective possession of territory to which the League considers it not to be entitled or in other ways defying the general verdict of the League does not appear to be clearly contemplated. It is true that such cases might finally, under the other provisions of the Treaty, result in the recalcitrant State resorting to war, but in such a case any prompt use or threat of the economic weapon would scarcely appear to be in accordance with the Treaty. Apparently, too, the article does not contemplate the weapon being used against a non-Member country which resorts to war,[1]

[1] The League's sanctions may be used against a non-Member country in certain circumstances, but the article which provides for this is Articles XVII not Article XVI.—Ed.

though it may be used, where a Member resorts to war, to prevent intercourse between that country and a non-Member.

(*b*) The economic weapon is only to be used against a country which has already been deemed to have committed an act of war against all other Members of the League and against which, therefore, the military and naval forces, as well as the economic weapon, may properly be used. The use of military and naval forces on the one hand or the economic weapon on the other, is therefore a matter of expediency and does not represent any difference in the relations of the League to the offending State.

(*c*) There is, however, one important difference between the two forms of pressure. Where a Member of the League resorts to war in disregard of specified Covenants, all other Members of the League are by the Covenant itself specifically obliged to apply the economic weapon. They are not similarly obliged to use their military or naval forces. In the latter case, the article only provides that it shall be the duty of the Council in such cases to *recommend* to the several Governments concerned what effective military or naval forces they shall severally contribute.

(*d*) The article clearly contemplates that so far as possible the responsibility for enforcing economic pressure shall be decentralized; i.e. a primary responsibility rests upon each Government to take action so far as its own nationals and own national machinery are concerned, arrangements being made by each of them separately and not by a single international authority.

WHY ACTION IS REQUIRED BY THE CENTRAL AUTHORITY
    OF THE LEAGUE

At the same time it appears to be clear that duties must fall upon the central governing body of the League and its permanent organization, if the weapon is to be effectively and efficiently used, for the following reasons :—

(e) The article requires action to be taken to prevent States which are not Members of the League (and on whom, therefore, no responsibility rests under the Treaty) from trading with the offending State. It clearly requires co-operative action on the part of the Members of the League to give effect to this provision.

(f) The action of an individual national Government would doubtless be in many respects assisted by a knowledge of the action which other Governments intended to take in execution of their duty under the article. General uniformity in the legislative and administrative provisions of the different States would be of great assistance to each particular Government in defending its action to its own national commercial interests which are affected. The sense both of justice and unity of effort would be increased and the general blockade would be more efficient. To secure this end, however, preliminary work of co-ordination is obviously required.

(g) In addition, some central action will doubtless require to be taken in order to see that certain Members of the League are really in a position to carry out their duty effectively. Supposing, for instance, that a single Balkan State was the offending party and that America,

Great Britain, France, and other distant Powers effectively prevented their nationals from trading with that State. The first effect would be that trade would be thrown into an adjacent Balkan State which might be a loyal but not very competent Member of the League. A through traffic might then still grow up in such a way as to render the blockade ineffective, and at the same time to give an indefensible trade advantage to a particular country through the inefficiency of its administration.

(*h*) Co-operative action is also required in order to give effect to the provision that Members of the League will "mutually support one another in the financial and economic measures which are taken in order to minimize the loss and inconvenience" resulting from the blockade. The simplest method is normally the purchase of surplus exports, and the net loss might fall upon Members in the proportions in which they contribute to the general expenses of the League. The problem will often, however, prove very complicated.

In considering the measures that will require to be taken it is necessary to reckon with the possibility that certain countries (in particular perhaps those contiguous with or adjacent to the offending State) will either not be Members of the League or, though Members, will be under a very great temptation to evade their Covenant duties or carry them out inefficiently, partly in consequence of their naturally closer economic relations with the offending State and partly because of the immediate danger of armed invasion from that State.

METHODS OF ECONOMIC PRESSURE

In these circumstances the experience of the late war suggests that the following main classes of action may have to be taken:—

(*i*) The severance of financial relations. This is the promptest and most effective immediate measure and also the one which in proportion to its effects is likely to cause least general economic loss. It is probably, therefore, the one which will be used first. At the same time it is one which eminently requires previous preparation and agreement.

(*j*) Export and Import prohibition by each loyal Member. This is the main economic weapon. It would be applied by means of a licensing system enforced through the national Customs Authorities. Its main difficulty is in determining destination and the danger that articles obtaining the licence for one destination may really be intended for reshipment or re-railage to the blockaded country, or at least that they might have the effect of making it more possible for the country of destination to export its own home produce to the offending State.

(*k*) Special measures in relation to States contiguous with and adjacent to the offending State. The main action taken during the war was the enforcement of a rationing system, i.e. limitation of imports into contiguous countries on such a scale as to render it extremely difficult for such a country to supply the enemy country. The position will, however, be different in cases of action by League Members; for usually the adjacent country will either be a *loyal* Member, in which case the enforcement of a rationing system would be an extremely invidious step, or it will be a *disloyal* Member, in which case the full blockade will presumably be enforced against it. In the third possible case of the adjacent country not being a Member of the League, it will be more in the position of a neutral in the late war, and perhaps the rationing system will be justifiable, the system being applied mainly under method (*j*) above and generally on the grounds adopted during the war.[1]

[1] It should be noted, however, that the rationing system, equitable and efficient as it was, rested on slender legal foundations. The relevance of statistical evidence as a reinforcement of specific evidence of enemy destination was in effect accepted by the British Court in the *Kim* Judgment, in September 1915: and in the *Baron Stjernblad* case in November 1916, the Prize Court, and afterwards the Privy Council, held that, although specific evidence of enemy destination was lacking, yet statistical evidence of excessive imports justified the Crown in detaining the goods pending enquiry. Thus, the Crown did not have to pay damages for detention, and the principle was established that in such cases the burden of proof was shifted from the Crown to the consignee. But the goods were not held liable to condemnation as prize solely on the ground that the commodity in question had been imported in abnormal quantity into the ostensible country of destination.

The Allied blockade measures were embarrassed by this absence of a rule which would justify the Prize Court in accepting statistical evidence as sufficient ground for seizure. But on the other hand, an importer in, say, Sweden might be genuinely in need of the goods he imported from overseas, even though his neighbours had already imported far more than the average requirements of the country, for re-export to Germany.

The Allies' difficulty was circumvented, partly by agreements with organizations of importers in the neutral States, but chiefly by the system of "Letters of Assurance," which were given in respect of advance bookings of shipments. By this means, the rationing principle could be applied without recourse to the Prize Courts.

Thus the legal sanction for the rationing principle is far from

The case that requires special consideration is that of a Member of the League whose loyalty or the efficiency of whose administration is subject to serious strain through the closeness of its economic connections with the offending country, or still more through the danger of invasion by that country. In order to meet this situation it will probably be necessary for the League to have officers of its own in each of the adjacent countries who would be watching on behalf of the League as a whole the way in which that country carried out its engagements.

Where such a country is threatened with invasion, the efficiency of any such measures must be dependent upon the other measures taken by the Members of the League to protect the loyal Member. In any case, the administrative task of a loyal Member with a long land frontier contiguous with that of the offending State will be one of very great difficulty. With no continuous military defence the extra inducements to smuggling across the border are likely to prove too much for the ordinary Customs arrangements. It would appear, therefore, to be the duty of each State with such frontiers to consider what special arrangements they should make to strengthen the Customs examination service when the emergency arises.

being as complete as a blockading power might wish; but the principle appears so much more equitable and efficient than its alternative, viz. the old method of relying on specific evidence of enemy destination for each shipment withheld—that it seems likely to commend itself again if ever the problem of restricting shipments to countries adjacent to a Covenant-breaker should arise. And then, if not before, the legal problem would have to be considered.—ED.

(*l*) Search by Naval Forces. It is obviously desirable on many grounds that the measures taken should require the employment of this weapon as little as possible. Generally, it will be used to supplement deficiencies of the other measures taken and as a last safeguard. The existence of sufficient naval forces will doubtless be the fundamental condition of the efficiency of the action taken as a whole, but the direct employment of these forces will doubtless be limited as much as possible.

(*m*) In addition, there are a number of supplementary, subsidiary, safeguards and precautions, the use of which will necessarily vary considerably according to the particular nature of the emergency, and the situation, character, and power of the offending State. Among these the most important is perhaps the cable and mail censorship. With the whole world as a possible supplying source it will perhaps always be difficult to enforce an efficient blockade without the use of this weapon, but it is clearly one which it is desirable to avoid as far as possible.[1]

In close connection with such action there are a

---

[1] It would be a mistake to assume that the weapon of censorship of cables and mails could again be used with anything like the effectiveness with which Britain was able to use it in the last war. It happened then that all Germany's ocean cable communications except two could be brought under British control: and of those two one was cut and the other diverted. It is remotely im probable that such a situation could be repeated unless by an immense combination of States such as the League should afford.

But even the largest combination could hardly expect to repeat what the Allies were able to do in that war in control of communications: for the developments of wireless and of aviation have radically altered the technical conditions.—ED.

number of supplementary measures, such as "black listing" and the formation of "stop lists," to which the same general considerations may apply.

One general remark on these methods of action must be made. The blockade preparations made by the central authority of the League will necessarily be known to all Members of the League. It is to be anticipated that the military authorities of the several Governments will be careful to adjust their own arrangements to these preparations. This will certainly render the imposition of an immediately effective blockade much more difficult, in case a Member of the League *does* "resort to war."

ORGANIZATION REQUIRED

This, then, is the general nature of the problem requiring consideration. In dealing with it it is necessary to distinguish clearly between

(1) the measures required, and the machinery through which they should be taken, *during the period of peace* in which preparations have to be made for an emergency not yet arisen, and

(2) the measures required, and the machinery through which they should be taken, *when the emergency actually occurs.*

A BLOCKADE INTELLIGENCE COMMITTEE

It is probable that, for the preparatory period, an International *Blockade Intelligence Committee* is required. This Committee would consist of officials connected with the Blockade Administrations of the different countries, and should, it is suggested, sit continuously or for a long period as soon as the League Organization commences to work. Its duties would be to consider what information must be available in order to enable blockade measures to be effectively taken (and to be effectively supervised centrally) when the emergency arises; what machinery is required to secure this; and to what extent existing information and arrangements for securing information are defective. It should include within its scope of enquiry the question of associating, either in time of peace or immediately on the outbreak of war, international League representatives with the administration of the national Governments, or certain of them. It would perhaps be well that the members of this Committee should remain primarily officials of their several Governments and should be paid as such, but that they should meet at the Headquarters of the League and, as a Committee doing League work, should have any special allowances, including subsistence, paid by the League. It would appear appropriate that, in order to link their work with the League and to emphasize the international character of their duties, the Committee should be presided over by an international official.

It might perhaps be well to arrange that every Member of the League should at once appoint one official (with substitutes to take his place where necessary) who would be available for work on this Committee, but that the Committee itself should immediately consist first of the officials of the five countries entitled to permanent membership of the Council of the League, with the proviso that these five at their first meeting should consider from what other countries (not being less than four in number) they should immediately invite officials to sit with them, the choice of these countries being subject to the approval of the Council of the League. It might be well, while providing that there should always be four such minor countries represented, that these four might vary from time to time.[1]

AN EXECUTIVE BLOCKADE COMMITTEE

Immediately upon a decision to use the economic weapon, it would be desirable that an *Executive Blockade Committee* should be at once summoned. This Committee might be constituted on the same general lines as the Blockade Intelligence Committee, except that its members should be of higher authority and perhaps consist of persons like the Blockade Ministers or Under-Secretaries of the several countries. For the efficiency of the Blockade it would be desirable that the Committee should consist of persons who would normally be able to speak finally for their Governments and secure that agreed action were taken. It is desirable that the several Governments should nominate their representatives for this Committee in time of peace, and keep their nominations continually up to date, so that the Committee can be at once summoned without any delay when the emergency arises. Such a Committee would doubtless work directly under the Council of the League, which at such a time would probably

[1] The Council of the League, as originally designed under Article IV, paragraph 1, of the Covenant, was to consist of representatives of the five "principal Allied and Associated Powers, together with representatives of four other Members of the League."—ED.

be in continuous session. It would be a matter for special consideration how far the assent of the several Governments at such a time should be obtained by direct communication between the members of the Committee, or through the Members of the Council.

A BLOCKADE COMMISSION

The Council and the Assembly, instead of at once authorizing the appointment of the Blockade Intelligence Committee, and arranging for the appointment of the Executive Blockade Committee when the emergency arises, may prefer as a preliminary measure to appoint at once a *Blockade Commission* (with membership similar to that of the second) in order to consider the general plan of the arrangements, including the proposals made above.

POSTSCRIPT

THE proposal made at the end of the foregoing paper, for the appointment of an International Blockade Commission to study Article XVI, was afterwards adopted.

In August 1920 the League Council considered the subjects dealt with in the paper, and decided to invite the First Assembly to appoint an International Blockade Commission. A Blockade Commission was accordingly appointed by the First Assembly in 1920, and reported to the Second Assembly in 1921.

But by 1921 the situation in regard to sanctions and the whole principle of collective security had become very different from what it was two years earlier when the paper was written. For by this time the United States Senate had rejected the Versailles Treaty and the Anglo-American Treaty of Guarantee to France (March 19, 1920); and the effect of this had been to stimulate British anxiety about sanctions and French anxiety about security. Great Britain now saw a prospect of challenge from the United States if naval force had to be contributed for the League's service. France, deprived of her expected treaty of guarantee, and seeing the whole system of collective security weakened, had made a military agreement with Belgium and an alliance with Poland. Italy and the Powers of the Little Entente had likewise made alliances: Europe was reverting to the pre-war system of exclusive alliances against private enemies in place of the League's system of reciprocal guarantees against the common enemy, war.

Furthermore, the Scandinavian States had united in demanding amendment of the Covenant so as to reduce the danger to which they might be exposed, whether from invasion or from severance of their chief trade connections, if they had to join in applying sanctions. Switzerland, too, had made anxious reserves about her neutrality.

And so, when the Second Assembly in 1921 formulated

its nineteen Resolutions about sanctions, its interpretations were such as to weaken, instead of to strengthen, the prospect of Article XVI being effectively applied. Faith in the League's sanctions seemed to have reached "low-water mark."

In 1922, however, some return to the principle of collective responsibility began to be traceable. The Third Assembly passed "Resolution XIV," which declared that security and disarmament are bound together.

In 1923 came the abortive Treaty of Mutual Assistance, which again tied together disarmament and security, and which, unlike the treaties of alliance against particular States, was in principle directed against any potential aggressor, whoever he might be.

1923 also saw an Assembly resolution, unanimously accepted except by Persia, defining the interpretation of Article X of the Covenant.

Lastly, in 1924—the date of the paper which follows—came the Geneva Protocol. The principle of "pooled security" was now fully reaffirmed, and for a short time support for the principle of sanctions seemed to have reached "high-water mark."   ED.

CHAPTER X

ECONOMIC SANCTIONS AND THE GENEVA PROTOCOL

Editor's Foreword

THIS paper was written on September 30, 1924, just before the Geneva Protocol was endorsed by the Fifth Assembly (October 2, 1924).

The Protocol expressly called for study of the League's economic and financial sanctions. Article XII said, "The Council shall forthwith invite the economic and financial organizations of the League of Nations to consider and report as to the nature of the steps to be taken to give effect to the financial and economic sanctions and measures of co-operation contemplated in Article XVI of the Covenant and in Article XI of this Protocol." So the author (being Director of the Economic and Financial Section of the Secretariat), wrote this paper as a first preparatory step towards meeting this requirement.

The Protocol would have modified the position concerning sanctions in important respects. In particular, by completing the abolition of the right of war between its signatories, it added to the kinds of war against which sanctions would be applicable: though the purpose of the agreement as a whole, with its provisions for comprehensive pacific settlement and for disarmament, was of course to reduce, not to increase, the danger that sanctions might have to be used.

Articles X and XI of the Protocol got round some serious difficulties which stand in the way of prompt and effective application of the sanctions of the Covenant (*vide* General Report on the Protocol, quoted page 52 League volume A14, 1927). Article XI gave an important interpretation of the obligations of Article XVI of the Covenant, which was afterwards used in Annex F of the Locarno Treaties: and Article XII provided for the working out of the economic and financial sanctions. Article IV included a surprising provision that, if a dispute between two States has been referred to arbitration, and one of them passively refuses to carry out the decision given, then the other disputant may be authorized to go to war (in some sense as an agent of the community) "to enforce an arbitral or judicial decision given in its favour."[1]

Lastly, in Article XIII, the Protocol referred to the "contingent military, naval, and air sanctions provided for by Article XVI of the Covenant and by Article XI of the present Protocol" and authorized the Council to receive undertakings from States determining in advance the forces which they would be able to bring into action immediately for the purpose of such sanctions. Any partial military alliance between the signatories was to "remain open to all States Members of the League which may desire to accede thereto." (This was intended to remove the danger of the partial alliances which had been growing up.) Thus, it was claimed that the Protocol would have clarified the position as to sanctions, and facilitated their effective application; and that whilst it extended their scope in some respects, its total effect would be to reduce the danger of their having to be used.

---

[1] Cf. Article XIII, paragraph 4, of the Covenant, and Part 2 of the French Disarmament Plan of November 1932: *vide* also Baker, *The Geneva Protocol*, p. 31.

ECONOMIC SANCTIONS AND THE GENEVA PROTOCOL

SEPTEMBER 30, 1924

In attempting to forecast the outline of probable action by League Members against an aggressor under the Covenant and Protocol, it may perhaps be assumed that the following considerations will be of importance.

(*a*) Action must be *immediate, simultaneous, and impressive* in character. Obviously, the object is to make the offending country yield as quickly as possible. One of the most likely cases is that a country, while not prepared to face the collective action of League Members, doubts whether that action will in fact be taken and "calls their bluff." In such cases, immediate and simultaneous action may result in surrender, quickly and before great loss or disturbance has been caused.

(*b*) With the above consideration in mind, it will be desirable that the first action, while being sufficient to demonstrate determination, should be such as to involve the minimum loss and the *minimum of lasting consequences*; more expensive measures being taken subsequently only if they prove necessary.

(*c*) It is desirable that this first action should be as *uniform* as possible, particularly with a view to avoiding complaints by some States that the action of others is such as to be less effective and to involve less proportionate sacrifice. This requirement can be met to some extent by an agreement beforehand as to measures to be taken, and to some extent by consultation during the progress of action.

(*d*) Careful consideration is, of course, required of the *legal effects*, both national and international, of action taken: in particular, the effect upon contracts both as between Members taking part in the measures and in relation to neutral States. The most important questions of all, of course, arise in case of the necessity of a naval blockade.

With these considerations in mind, it is possible perhaps to conceive of action proceeding in the following three main stages:—

FIRST STAGE: NO "STATE OF WAR"

The stage in which there is no state of war: financial and economic relations are severed, but by purely civilian and internal measures such as the blocking of banking accounts and the prohibition of exports and imports to or from the offending country.

On two hypotheses—the first that all the countries, except the offending one, were taking these measures, and the second that all of these countries were sufficiently strong and competent to enforce the measures perfectly—this action would, of course, suffice for a complete blockade, and no naval measure would be necessary. It is obvious, however, that neither of these hypotheses is likely to be realized.

Nevertheless, it will probably be well to start with measures of this kind only, and even among them to distinguish two different classes of action, between which some interval of time (though perhaps only a short one) should be allowed for repentance. The first measures to impose should be those which can be applied most quickly and which, if stopped, would have caused least trouble and disturbance. The simplest of these are mainly of a financial character, particularly blocking of bank accounts, refusal of market facilities to the offending country, the stoppage of transactions in securities, etc. . . . It might be well to concentrate at first upon securing immediate, uniform, and simultaneous action of this kind by all Members. In the likely case of an offending country only attempting to "call the bluff" of League Members, this action would suffice, and perhaps not even the economic measures need be put into force. At a very short interval, however, economic measures imposed by civilian action should follow, if no surrender has taken place.

For the measures, both financial and economic, contemplated in this first stage, it is desirable that there should be agreement beforehand as to the main classes of action to be taken; and it would be desirable that legislation, either at the time of the ratification of the Disarmament plans or about the same time,[1] should give all Governments the power to put the measures into force immediately, if and when the Council should call upon Member States to apply the sanctions in accordance with the Protocol.

The main subjects requiring consideration under

[1] The Protocol was not to come into force until a certain number of ratifications had been received and until a plan for reduction of armaments had been adopted by a Disarmament Conference (Articles XVII and XXI). If the Disarmament plans were not carried out within a certain time, the Protocol was to become null and void.

this stage are blocking and control of enemy credits, blocking of dealings in securities, stoppage of market facilities of all kinds; possibly detention of enemy property, or at least prohibition of sales or mortgages or other such transactions; arrangements for custody of dividends or other payments due; prohibition of export, prohibition of import, and in general perhaps prohibition of "trading with the enemy."

From the first moment, too, certain international action and machinery will be required in order to follow the course of the action, to co-ordinate it so far as practicable and desirable, and to consider whether and when the different States should be recommended to pass from the financial measures to the economic measures within this stage, and, more important, to pass from Stage I to Stage II if that proves necessary.

With this purpose, probably

A Blockade Council of people of the authority of Blockade Ministers should meet, directly the Council calls for sanctions to be put into force, and should be in practically permanent session until the action is terminated.

This Blockade Council should either be assisted by their own Blockade officials or perhaps by a Blockade Committee of officials working under the collective authority of the Blockade Council, as the Allied Maritime Transport Executive did under the authority of the Allied Maritime Transport Council during the war.

It would be the duty of this Blockade Council to arrange with and recommend to the different members the assimilation and regular development of their measures, and to advise the Council to recommend to Members the time at which it was desirable to pass to Stage II.

At the same time, the Intelligence Department of the League should be expanded; and the general statistics and information which are collected during peace to show the trade between all the countries should be supplemented by special study as to the imports and exports, particularly those of a vital character, of the offending country.

SECOND STAGE: STATE OF WAR BUT WITHOUT ACTUAL
    FIGHTING

If the above civilian measures are found to be insufficient, having regard to the completeness of the severance of intercourse with the offending country, and also to the power and will of that country to continue the struggle, the only recourse will be, in many cases, to proceed to the use of measures of external force, i.e. naval blockade. A vital consideration in passing to this stage will be to secure such a legal position that no neutral has any grievance in international law against the stoppage of its ship.

This will probably mean declaration of a state of war with the offending country on the part of at least those countries whose ships of war are allocated to stop forcibly the entry of merchant ships into the ports of the offending nation. It may prove desirable that this step should not, like the first one, be universal; that is to say, it may be desirable that some countries should be at war with the offending country while others (while enforcing economic boycott) are not.

THIRD STAGE: WAR IN THE FULL SENSE, INVOLVING
     COMBATANT ACTION

This stage should clearly only be reached if it proves unavoidable. One of the most likely occasions of this necessity would be the invasion by the offending country of a contiguous Member of the League which had severed economic relations. In this connection, it will be necessary to consider whether any form of exemption from the full normal obligations of economic sanctions, for example, at the decision of the Council, should be contemplated, as recommended by the International Blockade Committee of 1921.[1]

NOTE UPON CONTIGUOUS STATES

The danger of contiguous States, particularly if small and weak, will be one of the main practical problems in addition to the actual danger of attack by the offending State. There is, of course, the consider-

[1] The International Blockade Committee in 1921 recommended an amendment to Article XVI as follows:—"The Council may, however, at the request of a Member which can show that the facilities demanded are essential for its economic or political security, grant such exemptions as in its opinion will not conflict with the aims of Article XVI." After further discussion, the Second Assembly included this principle in its nineteen "Resolutions Concerning the Economic Weapon" (October 4, 1921) in the following altered terms: If it is thought desirable to postpone, wholly or partially, in the case of certain States, the effective application of the Economic Sanctions laid down in Article XVI, such postponement shall not be permitted except in so far as it is desirable for the success of the common plan of action or reduces to a minimum the losses and embarrassments which may be entailed in the case of certain members of the League by the application of the Sanctions." This was designed to meet the difficulties raised by the Scandinavian States.—Ed.

able administrative difficulty of preventing all trading when the financial inducements to the individual are so great as those created by increased war prices. It might be worth while to consider whether any information system can be contemplated to assist in dealing with this problem. Statistical information such as was the basis of rationing of neutrals during the war will doubtless be available in the Intelligence Department of the League, but this information will become incomplete unless it is supplemented by accurate and impartial information obtained during the progress of the action. The difficulties of arranging to appoint international consuls in such countries are obvious. It is possible, however, that the same system of information would serve to show whether exports were going from a contiguous State to the offending country and whether the first country was suffering through the absence of imports from the offending country in such a way as to make it desirable for other States to send in supplies of particular commodities.

POSTSCRIPT

DURING the autumn of 1924 the author continued his study of the steps to be taken to give effect to the financial and economic sanctions and co-operation contemplated in the Protocol and Covenant; but in November 1924 the British Labour Government fell, and in March 1925 the Protocol was rejected by the British Conservative Government, largely on account of its provisions about sanctions. That Government was averse from what it regarded as definite obligations for an indefinite contingency: instead of strengthening or clarifying general guarantees against breach of "the peace of nations," it preferred to restrict itself to "special arrangements to meet special needs."

There followed the Locarno Agreement of October–December 1925, which was such a "special arrangement to meet special needs," but which embodied some of the principles of the Protocol. Annex F of the Locarno Agreement contained, in a collective note to Germany, an interpretation, by the Powers concerned at Locarno, of the obligations of League Members under Article XVI of the Covenant: "The obligations resulting from the said article on Members of the League must be understood to mean that each State Member of the League is bound to co-operate loyally and effectively in support of the Covenant and in resistance to any act of aggression to an extent which is compatible with its military situation and takes its geographical position into account." This formula was derived from Article XI of the Protocol.

Almost simultaneously with the conclusion of the Locarno negotiations came a significant test of the League's peace-keeping powers—the Greco-Bulgarian incident which occasioned the next paper. ED.

CHAPTER XI

THE GRECO-BULGAR INCIDENT, 1925

Editor's Foreword

THE "Greco-Bulgar incident" of October 1925, when the League stopped an incipient war between Greece and Bulgaria, was not only an illustration of the value of the League's powers and organization for the prevention and stopping of war: it occasioned important innovations in the League's technique of peace-keeping and had considerable effect upon the League's subsequent development.

Fighting began on the wild and inaccessible Greco-Bulgar frontier: and on October 21, 1925, the Greek Government, at that time under the control of the military adventurer, General Pangalos, sent what amounted to an ultimatum to Bulgaria and began to invade the country. In days before the League existed Bulgaria would undoubtedly have gone to war: but now, drastically disarmed as she was, she had the League to appeal to. She ordered her frontier posts not to resist the Greek invasion by force, and early on October 23rd the Secretary-General of the League received the Bulgarian request, made under Articles X and XI of the Covenant, that the Council should be convened at once. That same morning, thanks to the existence of the League, an urgent summons to the Council was sent out and both disputants were reminded of their obligation not to resort to war till pacific procedure had been tried, and were urged to stay their hand pending the Council's meeting. This appeal reached them just—only just—in time to secure the calling-off of the Greek army's orders to attack and bombard a Bulgarian town.

Three days later the Council met. One part of its task —decision as to the merits of the case—could be deferred for the moment. The other part—stoppage of hostilities and withdrawal of troops—was of the utmost urgency. The Council called on Greece and Bulgaria to inform it within 24 hours that they had given unconditional orders for withdrawal behind the frontiers; within 60 hours evacuation was to be completed.

Bulgaria agreed. Greece, whose troops had by this time advanced a considerable distance into Bulgaria, hesitated for a critical day. Plans for constraint of a Covenant-breaker were there in a despatch-box. And then, realising no doubt that the League could and almost certainly would exercise compelling pressure against a peace-breaker, the Greek Government of General Pangalos also complied. By two o'clock on the 28th, officers representing the League were on the scene of the fighting, and by midnight of that day the last troops had been withdrawn.

Then, and only then, when the immediate danger had been averted, the Council turned to the other part of its task—to deal with the merits of the dispute. It sent another Commission to enquire and report: and within two months the net damages had been assessed, and had been paid by Greece, and the dispute was peacefully settled. Moreover, to prevent further troubles of the kind, the League appointed two officers of Swedish nationality, one for the Greek side and one for the Bulgarian.[1] Thus Greece and Bulgaria were restrained from doing each other grave and futile injury, without any party feeling aggrieved: a war very likely involving other Powers was averted: and, whilst it must be recognised that in this case the disputants were

[1] A year later Sir Arthur Salter was in Bulgaria and went down to the Greek frontier. "On arriving there I rather surprised the Bulgarian officers who accompanied me by saying that I proposed to walk over and invite the officer in command of the adjacent Greek frontier station to join us in our picnic lunch. The invitation was accepted after agitated telephoning to a higher Command, and I was able afterwards to take a photograph showing the League's Swedish officer, with a flag representing international authority, and the Bulgarian and Greek officers on either side of him."—ED.

both relatively weak States and the Great Powers relatively disinterested, yet it is fair to say that confidence in the League's collective system for the respect and preservation of "the peace of nations" was notably increased.

But this enhancement of prestige was not all that the League gained. Hardly less important was the fresh light thrown upon the League's problem and the fresh stimulus given to study of the League's powers for preventing breaches of the peace.

One of the chief consequences was an increase of faith in the imposed armistice and neutral zone as an instrument in the League's hands, both as a means of preventing the aggravation of situations dangerous to peace, and in the last resort as a help towards determining which of two disputants in such a case should be accounted a wilful aggressor. This lesson afterwards bore fruit in the League's Convention for Improving Means of Preventing War.

A further consequence was to stimulate consideration of the question—what authority can the League reasonably derive from its Covenant, both for the application of "conservatory" measures to prevent aggravation of critical situations and for the exercise of pressure to prevent war? For instance, if it were found desirable, in such a case as the Greco-Bulgarian one, to employ preventive measures such as a naval demonstration, before war had actually been resorted to, on what articles of the Covenant could such action be most soundly based? Could the League's action be based on Article XVI of the Covenant, although that article presupposes a "resort to war"? Or could it be taken under Articles X or XI? This is the problem examined in the following paper.

THE GRECO-BULGAR INCIDENT, 1925

OCTOBER 1925

At one stage of the Greco-Bulgar incident, it looked as if some means of pressure might have to be found by the Council.

It seems likely that (had the pressure required been against Greece) the Council would have wished to invite the Governments of Great Britain, France, and Italy to send ships off Athens, this naval demonstration being accompanied or followed by the withdrawal of Ministers by both these and other Member States.

This possibility led to unofficial discussions as to the form, and legal authority, under which, if the need arose, such action should be taken.

As the type of case illustrated in this incident may well occur, I think it worth while to put on record the views recorded with some comments.

ACTION UNDER ARTICLE XVI

It was urged on·the one hand that any measures involving real pressure, and in particular such a measure as the arrangement of a naval demonstration, should only be taken under Article XVI, the only article authorizing sanctions; and that therefore the proposed action should be specifically based on this article.

It was argued in support of this that the right of

the Council, under Article X, to "advise upon the means by which this obligation (that of respecting and preserving territorial integrity and political independence) shall be fulfilled," was only meant to cover measures short of sanctions, such as consultation between Governments and the exercise of diplomatic pressure. The same argument was applied to Article XI which, in case of war or threats of war prescribes that the League shall "take any action that may be deemed wise and effectual to safeguard the peace of nations."

The objections to this view seemed to be the following :—

(a) At the stage at which pressure might have been required, the Council might have found it difficult, and considered it impolitic, to declare that there had been "resort to war." Doubtless, Greece would have committed acts which Bulgaria might, on the ordinary principles of international law, have considered acts of hostility justifying resistance, which would have entailed war. But in the absence of such resistance it would have involved an important decision of principle to state that there had been "resort to war" (cf. Corfu case). Such a decision might in certain circumstances be necessary, but the Council would probably hesitate to take it, in the first instance, at a stage at which it desired to take no measures more drastic than the arrangement of a naval demonstration.

(b) In my view an even more serious objection is to be found in the fact that a declaration that

there had been "resort to war," and that, therefore,˷Article XVI was in force, accompanied
only by a naval demonstration, or by a demonstration plus the withdrawal of Ministers, would
have amounted to an implied abrogation of the
specific and unconditional obligation falling
directly upon all members under Article XVI
to sever, in such a case, "all trade and financial
relations," etc.

Now it may well be that, in applying Article XVI
when the time arrives, the Council may have to
modify, retard, and adjust the application of the
sanctions in accordance with the indications of the
1921 Assembly Resolution or otherwise.

But to take a decision at once implying the abrogation of the direct obligation, as an incident to the application of so simple a measure as a naval demonstration,
and without prolonged and careful consideration of the
consequences on the vital Article XVI, would surely
have been open to the gravest objection.[1]

The gravity of this objection is illustrated by a suggestion made by one member of the Council that

---

[1] This point was also made in the de Brouckère Report on
Sanctions (League papers A14, 1927, p. 70). "To say that ambassadors only will be recalled under an article" (XVI) "which
definitely requires the breaking off of all personal relations; to
say that certain commercial relations will be gradually severed
when the text demands that they should *all* be broken off *forthwith*, is to make an almost ridiculous use of a clause in which the
peoples most exposed to aggression see their supreme safeguard.
It means weakening it dangerously, and at the same time weakening the whole League."—ED.

economic sanctions were extremely expensive and onerous, and that, if sanctions were required, military and naval action would be preferable.

If by this was meant only a naval demonstration, the suggestion is sufficiently dealt with in the rest of this note. But if what he had in mind was more than this, i.e. that, if the demonstration were insufficient, the subsequent action should be, e.g. bombardment, without the general severance of economic relations, the following comments must be made.

(a) It seems contrary to the whole spirit of the Covenant, and especially Article XVI, that military action in this sense should precede, and be unaccompanied by, general economic sanctions.

The whole suggestion of the Covenant is "do what you can by economic pressure; supplement if necessary by military action."

(b) Apart from the intentions of the Covenant, the political importance of giving priority to economic pressure can hardly be overestimated: particularly as regards the United States of America and Great Britain.

(c) Apart from the general political advantage of economic pressure, there is this special consideration. Military or naval action means usually the action of one or two Powers. The objection to "giving the British Navy to the League," etc., would be immensely strengthened if the Navy were asked to take such drastic action as bombardment, while other Member States were not asked to suffer the economic loss involved in the stoppage of trade. Moreover, the moral authority behind such action would be much less. Action would be much more "Great Power action"; it would weaken the character of the League itself as an organ of collective, and as far as possible, equal world authority.

ACTION UNDER ARTICLE X

Again, it was suggested that the naval demonstration might be made under the powers of Article X. "The Council shall advise upon the means by which this obligation" (to respect and preserve against external aggression territorial integrity and political independence) "shall be fulfilled."

Greek troops were at the time undeniably in Bulgarian territory, and the immediate object of the pressure would have been to secure their withdrawal. The action would therefore appear to be specially relevant to the duty of preserving against external aggression. At the same time there were, in my view, the following objections to this course :—

(a) Article X is the most ambiguous, the most contested, and has been the most politically important of all articles in the Covenant.[1] It is specially important not to give it more than its uncontested meaning as an incident to action that could be properly based on other articles. I refer especially to the following ambiguities.

(b) Is it clear that "political integrity" is exactly

[1] See Postscript.—ED.

M

the same as "political inviolability"? Does it *necessarily* mean more than that Member States undertake that annexation shall not be secured by aggression? i.e. that they will see that the terms of peace involve restoration of territory. Now there was no suggestion in this case that annexation was intended.

(c) Is it not at least a tenable view that, the *principle* of preserving political territory having been posed in Article X, we must look to the subsequent articles to define the application of this principle? Can we not conceive a case, for example, in which, a dispute having taken place, the procedure of Article XV having been followed, the Council having been not unanimous, it would remain open to a Member without breach of the Covenant to take military action which would ultimately result in interfering with political integrity? Does Article X necessarily override the provisions as to the gap for freedom of action?[1]

I am not arguing as to which view is right. But is there not room for difference of opinion?

(d) There remain the arguments stated above as to the limited character of the "means" contemplated in Article X. I do not myself follow this argument so far as to think they would (if there were no other difficulties) exclude such action as a naval demonstration (see note as to Article XI under IV below), but they are worth bearing in mind.[2]

[1] I.e. Article XV, paragraph 7.—ED.   [2] See Postscript.—ED.

ACTION UNDER ARTICLE XI

Another suggestion, for which in my view the case is much stronger, was that the proposed action should be taken under Article XI. "Any war or threat of war . . . is hereby declared a matter of concern to the whole League, and the League shall take any action that may be deemed wise and effectual to safeguard the peace of nations. In case any such emergency should arise, the Secretary-General shall, on the request of any member of the League, forthwith summon a meeting of the Council."

It was under this article that the Council was summoned. Indubitably a threat of war existed. The phrase "any action, etc.," is wide. As to the arguments given above, it is difficult to say that so wide a phrase would not justify so restricted a measure as a naval demonstration.

At the same time, a naval demonstration in its essence is a threat of the possibility of something more. What is the "something more"? I think, indubitably, in view of the considerations set forth above, it should in the first instance have been economic pressure, not bombardment. I thought it would be well to suggest this in the original formula (see below).

But would even economic pressure be justified under Article XI alone? Personally, I am inclined to think at any rate the most drastic economic pressure would not. I believe there is *some* validity in the arguments above. I believe the natural and reasonable interpretation of "any action" under Article XI, in the context of the rest of the Covenant, is "any action short of such action as, in the case of an individual member of the League, would constitute an act of war or a resort to war." I think that, if the Council desires action of this kind to be taken, it should take it under Article XVI, and would only be justified in taking it if it felt able to say that the condition on which Article XVI comes into force—that there had been resort to war—was fulfilled.

In other words, I think a naval demonstration (which in itself is not equivalent to a resort to war, and is, indeed, not an act of war) would be justified under Article XI, and is best taken under that article;[1] but that, inasmuch as it is a menace of something more and that "something more" could only be taken under Article XVI, the original formula should contain a reference to Article XVI.

"GENERAL POWERS" OF THE COVENANT

Yet another suggestion was made: that the Council should act under the "general powers entrusted to it in the Covenant" without specifying any particular article or articles. The idea behind this proposal is that the Council should build up its powers by precedent and case law, which would be recognized as such by the Court of Justice, thus securing greater elasticity than is given by the written law of the Covenant.

I think this is a dangerous and very objectionable proposal, for the following reasons:—

(a) I think it is scarcely credible that it would be proposed if the aggressor were a Great Power.

[1] See Postscript.—ED.

The Council would in such a case certainly feel bound to base its action on a specific right contained in a definite text.

(b) The conception is very distinctly British and non-continental.

(c) It reflects, and would tend to develop, the conception of the League as a "European Concert," the Great Powers dominating the others and developing their own policy and rights. The rights of the small Powers depend on the sanctity of the written text.

A SUGGESTED FORMULA

The suggestion which I think the best results almost automatically from the above arguments. It is as follows :—

> In virtue of the provisions of the Covenant, in particular those of Article[s X and] XI, and in view of the possibility of action under Article XVI being necessary at an early date, the Council invites the Governments of Great Britain, France, and Italy to send ships of war to the proximity of the ports of Piraeus and Phalerum (but, pending further instructions, with due respect for territorial waters), in order that they may be in a position, if the necessity arises, to assist in the application of the economic sanctions which the Council may recommend in accordance with Article XVI.

On the whole I would prefer (for the reasons given under the heading "Action under Article X") to omit the words in *square* brackets, though I am a little uncertain on this. And on the whole I would prefer to retain the words in round brackets, though here again with some hesitation. The operation might be technically difficult—there might be difficulties of anchorage, for example. But until the Council is prepared to say that Article XVI is applicable, there is some advantage in its advising only such action as a country could take in accordance with the recognized principles of international law, without committing a hostile or questionable act.

SUGGESTED ACTION

Turning now from the formula to policy. I think the best further action for the Council to have taken, in addition to the above decision, would have been:—

(*a*) Simultaneously with the decision, to send the decision to all Member States, warning them of the possibility that they may soon be called upon to co-operate in the application of the provisions of Article XVI if the need should arise, and indicating that the Council would in that case continue its deliberations and communicate with them again.

It might have been well at the same time to communicate the decision formally to non-Member States (see below).

(*b*) If the demonstration were not immediately effective, to withdraw simultaneously all Ministers of all Council States, and so far as possible all other Member States (the Legation staffs, however, remaining). Neutral States, particularly United States of America, might have been invited to associate themselves in this action.

(c) For the Council to make definite blockade plans, inviting adjacent countries to co-operate; to appoint a Blockade Advisory Council; but, as to immediate practical action, to concentrate especially on *close sea blockade of Athens and its ports, Phalerum and Piraeus*, the remaining measures of economic pressure being applied gradually and with increasing stringency.

ADVANTAGES OF THIS POLICY

The advantages of the above procedure are:—

(a) It would avoid any action legally disputable.

(b) Measures involving serious loss would only be taken if absolutely necessary.

(c) It would secure the maximum of collective moral authority.

(d) The pressure on Athens, whose population would first see the combined fleet, and then, if necessary, directly suffer the loss of imports, would be rapid and overwhelming.

(e) There is one more advantage of the greatest importance. The great difficulty of effective blockade is the uncertainty as to America's action. It is difficult for a country like Great Britain to take at once definite action, such as the institution of a naval blockade, without knowing whether she will soon be faced with the dilemma of either stopping American ships under serious protest or going back on her decision. An answer from America on a purely hypothetical case could probably not be obtained. But if ships were sent, with a clear indication in the decision that, if necessary, the first action would be to institute a close blockade of a defined area, we should know the American attitude before taking the decisive step. And, what is equally important, we should have established conditions which would make it practically certain that this attitude would be favourable. The close blockade offers the least of difficulties from the point of view of international law and the American view of it. The nature of the dispute, the moral authority of the collective League decision, the character of the action immediately prepared, would make it certain that, at the worst, the American attitude would be—"we are a neutral; as a neutral we recognize the validity of blockade so established." Indeed, the American attitude would be likely to be more favourable, and to include a definite expression of good will if not actual co-operation, e.g. the passage of an "Act of Non-Intercourse." But even the adoption of the first of these positions by the United States would be an immense reinforcement and a source of additional strength for the future.

POSTSCRIPT

THE emphasis laid in this paper upon action to prevent war rather than upon action to stop war after it has begun was fully endorsed in the course of the League's later development.[1] It may be questioned whether some of the conclusions reached in the paper as to the legal authority for preventive action may not require some modification in the light of subsequent events.

Article X.—The author held that Article X is ambiguous: and he expressed some doubt as to whether such action as a naval demonstration could be taken under this article. Subsequent events have afforded support for this view. Certainly the article has proved "ambiguous," though the difficulty which (rightly or wrongly) prevented its effective use during the autumn of 1931 in the Sino-Japanese conflict did not happen to be one of those which the author foresaw in this paper. The Council appears to have assumed that it could do nothing under Article X except on the basis of an unanimous vote including the votes of the disputants: it could not advise about the means of preventing an aggression unless the State which might have been regarded as the aggressor would join in the vote. If this reading of the Covenant was sound, then, so far as action is concerned, "Article X makes the defendant a member of the jury" and "its provisions in fact seem to have only a moral value" (Morley, *The Society of Nations*, p. 89). It may be doubted whether the authors of the Covenant, especially President Wilson, meant the article to be thus stultified by the unanimity rule. Certainly, the author, writing in 1925, had not at that time had any reason to expect that the Council would find itself thus debarred from exercising under Article X that quasi-judicial function which the article appears to contemplate.

[1] E.g. the de Brouckère Report, League volume A14, 1927; and in the Rutgers Memorandum, February 1928.—ED.

Article XI.—There is also a difficulty about Article XI. The author held that a naval demonstration "would be justified under Article XI": but he did not deal with the question whether, on a legalistic reading of the Covenant, the unanimity rule would not prevent action of this coercive character from being taken *under this article*.

It may be disputable whether the unanimity rule should be applied to Article X: but it can hardly be questioned that the rule, if legalistically construed, does apply to Article XI. When the Council is acting under Article XI, as it was in the Greco-Bulgarian case and in the early stages of the Sino-Japanese case, it acts, not in a quasi-judicial capacity, but as an impartial conciliator; and except in matters of procedure, its decisions as a Council acting in the League's name require, it seems, a unanimous vote, *including the votes of the disputants* (Article V, paragraph 2), unless the disputants have agreed in advance to waive their right of veto under this article.

If the Council wanted to take such preventive measures as the sending of a fact-finding or peace-keeping Commission to a troubled area, it might hope to do so in many cases under Article XI with unquestionable legality.

In many cases, the disputants could be induced to agree to this course, as Japan ultimately did in 1931 in regard to the sending of the Lytton Commission: so that a unanimous vote would be secured.

In other cases, the Council might—by allowing itself some latitude in interpretation—treat (or threaten to treat) the sending of a Commission as a "matter of procedure," for which unanimity is not required. This was the line taken in the Greco-Bulgar dispute in 1925. The de Brouckère Report (A14, 1927) considered that "where there is no threat of war or it is not acute," a disputant might refuse consent to the Commission's visit, and that would suffice to block the Council's action under Article XI; but that where there is "an imminent threat of war," the Council may think it desirable "to send representatives to the locality of the dispute." In other words, in such a dangerous case, the sending of a Commission might be treated as a matter of procedure, and the unanimity rule thus circumvented.

A third way of ensuring that the unanimity rule shall not paralyse action under Article XI has been adopted in various treaties. In the Franco-German Arbitration Treaty of Locarno (1925) the parties undertook in advance to waive their right of veto under Article XI, and to accept peace-keeping measures recommended by the Council. The same provision was made in the General Act in 1928; and this was one purpose of the General Convention for Improving Means of Preventing War (1931) which originated from a German proposal in December 1927.

Fourthly, a majority of the Council's members might decide amongst themselves that peace-keeping action of a practicable kind ought to be taken by them in the public interest irrespective of the disputants' votes: they would be within their rights in doing so, even though their action were not based on any legally valid decision by the Council as a whole. This was done, for instance, by the "Twelve members of the Council" in the warning appeal addressed to Japan on February 10, 1932.

Lastly, the Council, after Article XI had been invoked, might declare itself competent to act under another article, e.g. Article XV. This was done in the Aaland Islands dispute in 1921: it was approved in principle by the Committees of the Council on March 15, 1927, and endorsep by the Eighth Assembly, September 26, 1927: and iu March 1932, after China had invoked Article XV, it had to be done despite the protest of Japan.

If, however, the Council, excluding the disputants, desires action of so coercive a character as a naval demonstration, it seems that it could not rely for the *legal* basis of its action upon a "Council recommendation" under Article XI. Its members, excluding the disputants, might act themselves, and might recommend action by others. Or alternatively, another article of the Covenant might be invoked. But there appears to be strong ground for the view that a step towards forcible constraint, such as a naval demonstration would be, could not be based *on Article XI alone.*[1]

But even if this be sound, it is but a slight and legalistic qualification of the author's main point, viz. that the League can and should undertake preliminary measures for the prevention of war before resort to war has taken place. The League's competence under the wide terms of Article XI is very extensive; and if the Council's members have the political will to act under this political article, a wide range of preventive action is undoubtedly open to them. That has been emphasized again and again in the League's statements and studies of the subject since the paper was written.   ED.

[1] For the distinction between preparing "conciliatory and pacifying" action under Article XI, and preparing coercive measures under Article XVI, see Rutgers Memorandum, February 1928 (C. A. S. 10, p. 33).—ED.

CHAPTER XII

IF THE UNITED STATES JOINED THE LEAGUE

Editor's Foreword

THE following letter was written to an American friend, who in November 1926 asked Sir Arthur Salter this question:

> "If the United States were a member of the League with a seat on the Council, what real danger would it run of being entangled in European political affairs against its will? As perhaps you know, the chief objection the average American has to the League of Nations is that he is afraid that, if the United States joins it, his country will be called upon to guarantee European settlements and become a party to European political intrigues. It may have to raise armies to send abroad to fight in quarrels which it considers none of its own and may run some danger of interference by the League in what this country considers its purely domestic affairs. I have been telling people that in my opinion these dangers were largely imaginary and that if the United States had a seat on the Council of the League no effective action could be taken without its consent. . . ."

IF THE UNITED STATES JOINED
THE LEAGUE

LETTER TO AN AMERICAN FRIEND, DECEMBER 1926

MY DEAR X. . . .

Now for the answers to your questions. The following is, I think, a fair and exact statement. It is certainly not affected by any conscious "propagandist bias."

LEGAL PRINCIPLES

(*a*) *Sovereignty.*—The fundamental principle on which the whole League is based is of course that it is an association between nations who retain their independent sovereignty and act by agreement only, and not an authority whose decisions the signatories have bound themselves beforehand to accept.

The *exceptions* are few, definite, and limited to:—

(1) The abandonment of the right to make war *either* without a process of prior enquiry, *or* in enforcement of a claim which has been adversely reported upon

> either (*a*) by *all* the members of the Council except the parties to the dispute (or all those members plus a majority of the Assembly if the case has been referred by the Council to the Assembly),
>
> or   (*b*) *if*, by an arbitration or judicial authority, and *if* the parties to the dispute have

agreed that the case is suitable for decision by such authority.[1]

(2) An undertaking by each signatory State to co-operate in an economic and financial blockade against any State (whether a Member of the League or in certain cases a non-Member), which *in the judgment of that signatory* State has resorted to war under conditions under which, as described in (1), signatories have undertaken not to resort to war.

This is, I think, an exact and comprehensive statement. But it is complicated and obviously needs further explanation. Let me approach the question from another angle.

(b) *Unanimity.*—Article V provides that "except where otherwise expressly provided in this Covenant or by the terms of the present Treaty, decisions at any meeting of the Assembly or of the Council shall require the agreement of all Members of the League represented at the meeting."[2]

Apart from such exceptions, therefore, America would obviously not be legally bound either to take part in an interference with other countries or accept any interference herself without her specific consent in the particular case.

What then are these exceptions to the unanimity rule? They are:—

[1] For the moral obligation to recognize certain classes of cases as suitable for decision by arbitration or judicial authority, see below.—A. S.

[2] This is of course precisely what makes the League an interstate, not a superstate, organization.—A. S.

(1) *"All matters of procedure* . . . including the appointment of Committees . . ."

As all this is merely a matter of preparing the material on which decisions will be later taken in accordance with the unanimity rule, it does not affect the main question.

(2) *Certain definite administrative tasks* of the League, e.g. decisions as to the execution of the Saar provisions; so too, by subsequent provision, execution of provisions of such Protocols as the Austrian, Hungarian, or Bulgarian.

These again obviously do not affect the main question.

(3) *Certain provisions in Articles X, XII, XIII, XV, and XVI.* I will deal later with Article X. The net effect of the other articles is, I think, correctly summarized in the earlier part of this letter. It will, however, be well to deal with these provisions in somewhat greater detail.

These are the only cases in which a State by signing the Covenant undertakes to take action or refrain from action.

Articles XII, XIII, XV, and XVI.—Under Article XII signatories undertake in no case to resort to war until three months after an award by arbitration or judicial decision.

This is not therefore an abandonment of the right to make war, but only of the right to make war without prior investigation.

Under Article XIII signatories undertake to submit disputes "which they recognize as suitable for submission" to arbitration or judicial settlement, and *in that case* they agree to carry out in full good faith any award or decision that may be rendered, and that they will not resort to war against a Member of the League which complies therewith. This obligation is dependent upon the agreement of the parties themselves that the case is suitable for decision by arbitration or judicial settlement. But, while remaining itself the judge on this point, each signatory State has committed itself to the declaration of general principle that

> "Disputes as to the interpretation of a treaty, as to any question of international law, as to the existence of any fact which if established, would constitute a breach of any international obligation, or as to the extent and nature of the reparation to be made for any such breach, are declared to be among those which are *generally* suitable for submission to arbitration or judicial settlement."

Signature therefore implies no absolute legal abandonment of the future right of decision, but that future right is affected by the moral obligation of the observance of the principle.

Under Article XV, signatories undertake to submit disputes which the parties do *not* agree to have settled under Article XIII for discussion by the Council. If the Council is unanimous except for the parties in dispute, the signatories agree that they will not go to war with any party to the dispute which complies with the recommendations of the report.

This is therefore a further restriction on the right

to make war, additional to the restriction of the right to fight without delay which is abandoned under Article XII. But it is obvious that, with a Council already of fourteen members, this provision could only apply against a country whose claim was incontestably ill-founded. If there was a division of opinion in the Council, signatories retain their freedom of action and every party in dispute is at liberty to resort to war, after waiting three months after the Council's report in accordance with Article XII. The same Article XV includes the important provision that "if the dispute between the parties is claimed by one of them, and is found by the Council, to arise out of a matter which by international law is solely within the jurisdiction of that party, the Council shall so report, and shall make no recommendation as to its settlement."

The above articles are those which affect the rights of a signatory to act in furtherance of its own rights. We now come to the articles (XVI and X) relevant to interference in other countries' quarrels.

Under Article XVI signatories undertake to subject a Member which has resorted to war in disregard of the above undertakings to a financial and economic blockade, and Article XVII extends the effect of this Article to cover a resort to war under similar conditions by non-Members.

This obligation falls direct on each signatory, which is itself judge of whether the *casus foederis* has arisen. No signatory undertakes to accept the judgment on this point of other States, or the Council.

Article XVI further provides that in such a case it

shall be the duty of the Council to "recommend" what effective military, naval, or air force the Members of the League shall provide. Each Government *decides* itself whether it will comply with such a recommendation; and as the Council, in making the recommendation, acts unanimously, it is obvious that it would only recommend such a contribution from a member of the Council as was acceptable to that member. The only importance of this provision, therefore, for the question we are now discussing, is that it may be taken to imply a moral obligation to supply *some* military, naval, or air contribution, the contributor remaining entirely free as to the character or amount.

Lastly, we come to *Article X*.

> "The Members of the League undertake to respect and preserve as against external aggression the territorial integrity and existing political independence of all Members of the League. In case of any such aggression, or in case of any threat or danger of such aggression, the Council shall advise upon the means by which this obligation shall be fulfilled."

This has been perhaps the most disputed article of the Covenant. It is certainly ambiguous. The last sentence of it is important. It clearly contemplates the possibility of diplomatic action resulting in the *withdrawal* of the aggressor from the invaded territory, as distinct from immediate expulsion by force. It is arguable that it doesn't so much deal with the question of immediate fighting (which is dealt with by the subsequent articles) as supplement them by an undertaking to secure that the terms of peace shall be such as to restore the frontiers. It is clearly subject to Article XIX which provides that "The Assembly may from time to time advise the reconsideration by Members of the League of treaties which have become inapplicable and the consideration of international conditions whose continuance might endanger the peace of the world."[1] It is arguable that it only lays down a general principle whose application and exact scope is defined by the subsequent articles.

In my personal view it is the only badly drafted and unnecessarily ambiguous article in the Covenant, and it has had a great deal too much importance attached to it. In any case, its ambiguity is such that it is better for any country desiring to know the exact character and limits of the obligations which it assumes by signing the Covenant to look rather to the other articles of the Covenant for the answer.[2]

---

[1] The provisions of Article X and Article XIX were originally intended to hang together. Up till a late stage in the drafting of the Covenant (i.e. in the "Cecil-Miller" draft) the text of the first part of Article X (the territorial guarantee) stood side by side in the same article as the principle of Article XIX (reconsideration of Treaties). The two provisions were separated in the "Hurst-Miller" draft, February 1–2, 1919. An attempt was afterwards made (February 6th) by the British delegation to get the principle of revision restored to its place in Article X, but this did not succeed.—ED.

[2] Great importance has been attached to this article. President Wilson declared to the Senate: "Article X seems to me to constitute the very backbone of the whole Covenant." Article X was the chief factor in the Senate's vote against the Covenant: and it was strongly criticized in Canada. Its fundamental importance was emphasized by many speakers in the Special Assembly of March 1932, which dealt with the Sino-Japanese conflict. Never-

PRACTICAL EFFECTS

So much for an analysis of the legal provisions. But I gather you are more interested in the question of what they amount to, and are likely to amount to in practice, in view of the actual working of the League. On this I will give you my own personal view for what it is worth.

Let me take your two points separately.

Possible Interference in American Affairs.—Formally, as we have seen, the position is clear. Matters which are by international law solely within the domestic jurisdiction of a State cannot even be the subject of recommendation (Article XV). On matters of international concern, nothing can be done affecting the action of a State without the consent of that State except in the case of resort to war. In the limited cases, defined above, in which action affecting the right to war can be taken without the consent of a State, there is formally no difference between signatories and non-signatories (Article XVII).

In practice, I think this clear formal position requires a little qualification. As regards "resort to war" in violation of the Covenant, the attitude of Members of the League towards a Great Power which was

theless, the actual course of the Sino-Japanese case affords strong support for the author's view as to the ambiguity of the article. The Council (rightly or wrongly) appears to have assumed that the unanimity rule must be strictly applied to Article X: so that it could not, under this article, decide that Japan had committed aggression, or "advise" as to the action to be taken, without the concurrent vote of Japan herself: if it be indeed the case that an aggressor can render the article nugatory by merely refusing to agree that he is an aggressor, then the article must surely be, as the author says, "badly drafted."—ED.

acting in deliberate breach of engagements which it had voluntarily taken might well be somewhat different from their attitude to one which had taken no such engagements.

More important, however, than the possible action of other countries is the moral obligation resting upon a signatory country itself to conduct its policy in accordance with the letter and spirit of the Covenant, and the pressure exercised on its Government by its own public opinion.

As an illustration, let me cite the general principle enunciated in Article VIII :—"Members of the League agree that the manufacture by private enterprise of munitions and implements of war is open to grave objections. The Council shall advise how the evil effects attendant upon such manufacture can be prevented, due regard being had to the necessities of those Members of the League which are not able to manufacture the munitions and implements of war necessary for their safety." There is no question of a signatory being committed by this article to any definite internal action, or to the acceptance of any external, i.e. collective, action affecting itself, without its consent. But a signatory has endorsed a general principle, and those of its own people who believe in that principle can press their views with a very powerful argument.

This is the main character of the effect of signature— the orientation of policy in the general direction indicated by the League and the reinforcement of those internal forces which are working in that direction. This must not be overstated, but it is much more important than any prior legal commitment to definite measures or to the acceptance of external views as to future definite measures. Indeed, as I have explained, such a legal commitment is practically non-existent.

Obligation to Interfere in External Affairs.—Much the same is true of this. A signatory is never committed to accept the verdict of other countries—even when they are unanimous—as to whether its interference in a particular dispute is required or not. At every stage a State not party to the dispute has the power to block action—and it remains sole and ultimate judge as to whether its own action should be taken.

But it does accept a prior obligation to take action if, in its own judgment at the time, its action is due in accordance with the terms of the Covenant.

The common American fear that America, by signing, would find herself committed, through the overriding opinion of other countries, to supporting a country which she herself might think in the wrong is unjustified. But the argument that she would morally be less free to stand out altogether of a dispute resulting in war is, I think, well founded.

The choice here, for a signatory, is between alternative risks and responsibilities. By coming in she adds to the forces which prevent war, she acquires a position which enables her to prevent the negotiations being so conducted as to enable the country which in her view is substantially in the wrong manœuvring itself into the position of the technical victim of aggression. But if in spite of this the war does come, she has a moral obligation which at least increases the chances of her participation. Conversely, by staying out, she increases the chances of a war in which she may be involved (as America was in 1917). Is the larger chance of participation in a less likely war preferable to a smaller chance of participating in a more likely war? That is the kind of question a country debating signature will ask. Some countries, e.g. Great Britain, are clearly right in thinking that the net result of signature is to reduce their chances of finding themselves at war. For the United States of America the answer is of course not so clear.

It should be added of course that the general disadvantage of war in the world even for non-belligerents is a further factor in the problem.[1]

GENERAL COMMENTS

A few general remarks to conclude. The Covenant is much more elastic in operation than can be realized if it is not seen in working. The American view in particular (which is generally over-legalistic from a European, or at least a British, point of view) has been grossly mistaken in reading the Articles as a series of provisions designed to be automatic in operation. Starting from this point of view, the drafting is criticized as failing to attain a kind of precision at which it is supposed to aim, but does not. On the contrary, the Covenant attempts and provides (with

[1] Cf. the American Government's Note to Japan and China, October 20, 1931, quoted on p. 249.—ED.

a skill which those who work under it admire more with every new experience which tests it) a procedure and a method by which the influence of its Member States can be brought to bear to settle particular disputes, and avert war, in accordance with certain *principles*, but with a variety of remedy and resource as changing as the difficulties to be dealt with.

The heart and centre of the Covenant is the fundamental obligation not to go to war except after an adequate interval—an interval used to bring the public opinion of the world to bear upon the public opinion of the intending belligerent. And the obligation to take collective action by "blockade" against a belligerent is limited to cases in which the belligerent has resorted to war without this interval—or in support of an ambition which is *universally* reprobated ("unanimity" apart from the "parties to the dispute").[1]

I have not dealt here with the question of participation in the League's technical work, etc. In my view an unwillingness to sign the political engagements is no reason at all for abstaining from association in such work.

Conversely, I have never agreed with League supporters who tend to argue—"You agree the League has done a useful work in Austria and Hungary which couldn't have been done otherwise—therefore you ought to sign." This is an obvious *non sequitur*. The conclusion is, not the acceptance of political engagements, but only the association with similar work.

The more important political problem must be judged on its own merits. The most important relation

[1] *Vide* paragraphs 6 and 7 of Article XV.—Ed.

between the two is that association with the technical work would lead to an understanding of how the League works in practice, which is an important element in judging the exact effect of the political commitments.

POSTSCRIPT

THE paper was written prior to the alteration in the American Government's attitude towards the League which began in 1927. For some indications of that change, as regards collaboration in the League's work for the organization of peace, see Footnote to Chapter IV, p. 57. As regards prevention of war, see Postscript to Chapter XIII. For a summary of the subject, see *The Approach to World Unity*, by Arthur Sweetser, League of Nations Association (of the United States of America), July 1929.

ED.

ARBITRATION, SECURITY, AND DISARMAMENT: FOUR NOTES

Editor's Foreword

THESE four papers deal with the four chief subjects of the important Resolution passed by the Eighth Assembly in 1927: they were written when the Arbitration and Security Committee set up at the instance of that Assembly had just held its first session.

SANCTIONS UNDER ARTICLE XI AND ARTICLE XVI

The first paper deprecates reopening discussion of Article XVI of the Covenant at that time, on the ground that this would probably lead to weakening the article. The occasion, and the reason, for this warning is explained by what happened in the Eighth Assembly.

The Assembly began with a clash of views. The French spokesman, always hankering after a return to the Geneva Protocol, urged that it was politically impossible to make progress in disarmament without further guarantees of security: for evidence of this, he could point to the deadlock in April 1927 in the Preparatory Commission for the Disarmament Conference and the breakdown in July of the Coolidge Naval Conference. The German spokesman urged, on the contrary, that it was useless to wait till an ideal security had been achieved and that general disarmament was the most urgently needed contribution to true security for all. The British spokesman's contribution was negative. His country, he claimed, had already gone far on the road of unilateral disarmament; her peculiar position in the British Commonwealth debarred her from accepting arbitration in advance; and as for collective security, to ask her, when she had already accepted the special responsibilities of Locarno, to give such guarantees for other frontiers, "would be asking nothing less than the disruption of the British Empire."

Thus it was evident that British opposition to any *general* application of the principle of "pooled security" was particularly strong at that time (cf. also the British Memorandum to the League on Arbitration and Security, January 1928). It should be remembered, too, that at this date the Kellogg Pact had not yet been proposed, and nothing had yet been said (such as Mr. Stimson's declaration of August 8, 1932, about American neutrality) which might have relieved British anxiety as to American opposition in the event of sanctions having to be applied with a backing of British naval force.

Hence the warning in the paper.

The Eighth Assembly, despite its difficult start, finally reached important agreements of principle in a long Resolution on arbitration, security, and disarmament. It was this Resolution which began with the well-known declaration of the principle of collective security, viz. that "the principal condition" of the success of the disarmament work "is that every State should be sure of not having to provide unaided for its security by means of its own armaments and should be able to rely also on the organized collective action of the League of Nations."

The Resolution said further that the League's collective action "should aim chiefly at *forestalling or arresting* any resort to war, and if need be at effectively protecting any State victim of aggression." In thus emphasizing the importance of preventive action, the Assembly was following the lead strongly given in papers prepared by the Committee of the Council in 1926–27. (Cf. the de Brouckère Report, December 1926, and the Report approved by the Council, March 15, 1927. League Volume A14, 1927.)

The Resolution also recognized the need for further clarification of the position in regard to sanctions. The burdens of collective action, it said, would be the more readily accepted by States "in proportion as (*a*) they are shared in practice by a greater number of States; (*b*) the individual obligations of States have been more *clearly defined and limited.*" A sequel to this was the Rutgers Memorandum of February 1928 (C.A.S. 10), which is now the most recent and authoritative study of Articles X, XI, and XVI of the Covenant. This was prepared for the Arbitration and Security Committee set up at the instance of the Eighth Assembly.

Besides this Resolution, the Eighth Assembly passed a Resolution proposed by Poland, declaring that "a war of aggression can never serve (ne doit jamais servir) as a means of settling international disputes and is in consequence an international crime," "that all wars of aggression are, and should always be, prohibited," and "that every pacific means must be employed to settle disputes of every description which may arise between States."

ARBITRATION, SECURITY, AND DISARMAMENT: FOUR NOTES

DECEMBER 20, 1927

An attempt to add anything substantial to the provisions of Article XVI (apart from the ratification of the two amendments already recommended by the Assembly)[1] would be very dangerous at present. It

[1] The two amendments referred to were:—

(1) Recommended by Fifth Assembly, 1924:—
    Latter part of first paragraph of Article XVI shall read as follows: "which hereby undertake immediately to subject it to the severance of all trade or financial relations and to prohibit all intercourse at least between persons resident within their territories and persons resident within the territory of the Covenant-breaking State and, if they deem it expedient, also between their nationals and the nationals of the Covenant-breaking State, and to prevent all financial, commercial, or personal intercourse at least between persons resident within the territory of that State and persons resident within the territory of any other State, whether a Member of the League or not, and if they deem it expedient, also between the nationals of that State and the nationals of any other State, whether a Member of the League or not."

(2) Recommended by the Sixth Assembly, 1925:—
    In the second paragraph of Article XVI delete the words in brackets. "It shall be the duty of the Council (in such cases) to recommend to the several Governments concerned what effective military, naval, or air force the Members of the League shall severally contribute to the armed forces to be used to protect the covenants of the League."

Neither amendment has yet (February 1933) received the ratifications necessary to bring it into force.—ED.

would probably have not merely a negative result but would end in *weakening* the force of the present article.

It must be remembered (*a*) that the present text was *drafted* by the Allied Powers, although *accepted* by those who suffered most by blockade; and (*b*) that it was agreed to on the assumption that America would be a member of the League, an assumption of vital importance in regard to Article XVI, particularly in the eyes of a country like Great Britain. In some countries, certainly in Great Britain, the atmosphere is probably as unfavourable now for the discussion of the sanctions of Article XVI as it was in 1921; and it is likely that a renewed examination would again give us a similar result; that is, the examination would consist in interpreting away and adding reserves to the provisions, not in strengthening them.

There are two principal features in Article XVI which on the one hand make continental countries think it gives insufficient security, and on the other hand are to Great Britain valuable limitations of what would otherwise be an excessive responsibility. These are (*a*) the fact that each country remains the ultimate judge as to whether it has an obligation to fulfil under the article in any given case, and (*b*) the fact that, unless unanimity (minus the vote of the disputants) is secured, every country is free to take its own course.[1]

1 "Free to take its own course," i.e. free, under the conditions of Article XV, paragraph 7, to go to war in the last resort without becoming liable to sanctions. It may be questioned whether the keeping open of this conditional right of war, free from sanctions, really would reduce the danger that sanctions might have to be used. When the Amendments to the Covenant, designed to close the gap, were discussed in 1930, the British Delegation maintained

As regards the first of these limitations, it seems hopeless to expect that anything more can be secured at present than the renewed understanding (contained in the 1921 Resolutions) that the Council should recommend the date of the application of sanctions.[1]

As regards the second, the discussions of the last three years have shown the difficulties in closing the "gap" completely by direct and general action. To some extent countries desiring to do so can reduce it by action *inter se* without any general agreement, simply by the process of concluding all-in arbitration agreements; for it would obviously be much less likely that the Council would fail to agree as to the country in fault in case of war between two countries, one at least of whom must have broken an arbitration treaty.

If, however, Article XVI offers no line of advance, Article XI may afford a real bridge between the two opposing points of view. Much useful work has been done in the last few years in exploring the opportunities given by this article. It would be well that this work should continue, and it is essential that it should be borne in mind on all relevant occasions.

that this danger would in fact be reduced if the gap were closed: and that view was endorsed by the Committee of Eleven which drafted the Amendments.—Ed.

[1] The third of the Amendments proposed by the Assembly of 1921 read thus:—

"The third paragraph of Article XVI shall read as follows:—'The Council will notify to all Members of the League the date which it recommends for the application of the economic pressure under this article.' "—Ed.

Under Article XI, any kind of action may be taken when peace is threatened, except, I imagine, what amounts to an act of war.[1] In practice, both in the actual case of Greece and Bulgaria and in any likely case which we can conceive, the first measures would be likely to be under this or the similar articles (Articles X, XII, XV). This enables an elastic and graduated action carefully adjusted to the needs of a particular case at each stage of the negotiations. It has the enormous advantage that an effective pressure can be exerted without declaring that the conditions exist under which Article XVI must automatically come into force, and therefore without either destroying the plain meaning of Article XVI or exposing all the countries concerned to the expensive and wasteful action and long enduring results of economic blockade.

A more detailed study of the possible alternative means of action—withdrawal of Legations, naval demonstrations, etc.—would increase the sense of security, without involving any new binding engagement on members, and without purporting to contain any exhaustive statement of the means of action open to the League; for it would show that the League had at hand a considerable armoury of alternative weapons without in any way depriving itself of the power to improvise others at the moment of actual need. The knowledge that a scheme of alternative or successive means of pressure had been examined beforehand will increase the belief that the League

[1] It may be questioned whether this is not rather too extended an interpretation of the League's powers under Article XI. See Postscript to Chapter X.—Ed.

will act if the need arises, and when the time comes this knowledge will assist the League in doing so.

Such a scheme would in this way strengthen the League's sanctions. At the same time it might be presented in a way very attractive to Powers like Great Britain, for the following reason. The more the emphasis of League action is based on the period *prior* to that at which Article XVI obligations mature, the less is the chance of the latter obligations having to come into force. In most cases, an aggressor can be stopped on the one vital condition that he is convinced that the whole of the rest of the League world is prepared definitely to act against him. The actual application of Article XVI would do this at a tremendous cost and with long-enduring results, but any measure involving collective and practical action would be equally effective in deterring the would-be aggressor. The building up of Article XI policy has therefore for Great Britain the great advantage that it enormously reduces the chance of her being obliged to apply the sanctions of Article XVI under an engagement by which she recognizes she is bound but which she feels to be a very onerous one.

Article XI procedure has other advantages, including that of giving time during which negotiations could take place with regard to the attitude of third parties (e.g. United States of America), if the earlier procedure should be ineffective. This again is a great and perhaps decisive advantage in the case of Great Britain, who may always be expected to hesitate seriously about any measure under Article XVI which might involve a war with the United States, or a war with the aggressor under conditions which would involve serious and continual friction with the United States as a neutral on blockade points.

FINANCIAL ASSISTANCE TO THE VICTIM OF AGGRESSION

I notice that a decision of the recent Committee of the Council mentions this scheme in a context which suggests, though not decisively, that it was contemplated simply as one of the measures to give effect to Article XVI.[1] This question was discussed at some

[1] This point proved to be the most controversial of all the questions raised during the four and a half years of discussion of the Convention of Financial Assistance. Might the League's financial assistance be assured to a State *threatened* with attack, or might it only be used after war had actually been resorted to? When the paper was written the position was as follows:—Finland had proposed, in May 1926, the preparation of a scheme of financial assistance to States victims of aggression: and in December 1926 the Council, on the advice of its Committee, had asked the League's Financial Committee to prepare such a scheme. "Having regard to the financial assistance provided for in Article XVI of the Covenant, to ask the Financial Organization of the League to consider the Finnish proposal and all other similar measures, with a view to the establishment of a common scheme of financial assistance in support of a State which is the victim of aggression." The Financial Committee accordingly worked out a scheme, which the Eighth Assembly approved in principle. Up till the end of 1927, when the present paper was written, the suggestion that the financial assistance might well be used *before* resort to war had occurred and before Article XVI came into play appears not to have been clearly brought out.

.   .   .   .   .

But shortly after the paper was written, in February 1928, M. Rutgers, in his Memorandum for the Arbitration and Security Committee, strongly supported this idea (C.A.S. 10, p. 39), and the Ninth Assembly, which was asked to give a ruling on the subject, provisionally endorsed it. A draft Convention was

length in the Committee of the Council, when it was
made quite clear that the reference to Article XVI
which is contained in 7 (*b*) of the Council resolutions
of December 8, 1926 ("having regard to the financial
assistance provided for in Article XVI") was not
accepted as limiting the scheme to that Article. It
seems to me that having regard to the arguments
above, it is of the utmost importance that the
scheme should be approved in a form which enables
the Council to use it among the Article XI measures,
that is, in the preventive stage, before it is claimed
that the conditions have arisen which compel every
loyal member to put into force the full Article XVI
action. I can conceive no better action for demon-

accordingly submitted to the Tenth Assembly, providing for
financial assistance to any League Member, signatory of the
Convention, who by a unanimous vote of the Council was held
to be a victim of, *or threatened by*, aggression. But the Tenth
Assembly (1929) proved to be strongly divided on the subject.
It was objected that, if the Council were to grant financial assistance before war occurred, its position as an impartial mediator
might be compromised. Finally, after much discussion, the
Eleventh Assembly in 1930 agreed upon a formula to reconcile the
two views. "If the Council . . . shall, in any international
dispute likely to lead to a rupture, have taken steps to safeguard
peace . . . and if one of the parties shall refuse or neglect to
conform to such steps, the Council may, at the request of the
other party . . . grant financial assistance to the last-named
party, *provided it considers that peace cannot be safeguarded otherwise.*"
In other words, financial assistance may be used as a preventive
instrument, but the Council must first take every possible step to
secure agreement between the disputants.

As a further guarantee against abuse, the party to whom
financial assistance is granted has to undertake, for his part, to
submit the dispute to peaceful settlement and to conform to any
peace-keeping measures recommended by the Council.—ED.

strating to the aggressor that there is a collective determination to act together against him, if necessary by Article XVI measures, than the issue of a guaranteed loan for the victim. In the many cases in which such a demonstration would result in the withdrawal of the aggressor, we should have avoided the irreparable consequences of the application of Article XVI.

In suggesting this I am not implying that the countries agreeing to the financial assistance scheme should be asked to put their guarantee at the disposal of a majority vote as distinct from a unanimous vote of the Council (minus the disputants).[1] Nor do I suggest that to put the scheme into operation would imply that the members were expected to apply economic blockade at that moment. On the contrary, it would normally imply that Article XVI sanctions should wait until it was seen if the earlier measures were successful. Nor on the other hand need the fact that the scheme was available under Article XI prevent it being continued on to the Article XVI period or being initiated in such a period if for any reason it had not been found expedient to use it in an earlier stage.

TEST OF AGGRESSION

Difficult as the problem of the test of aggression is, I believe it has been exaggerated. Both those who oppose any attempt to find new tests of aggression,

[1] The Convention provides that decisions of the Council as to granting the financial assistance "shall be taken by the unanimous vote of the members represented at the meeting, the votes of representatives of the parties to the dispute not being counted in determining such unanimity" (Article XXVIII).—ED.

and those who regard them as necessary, appeal to the extreme difficulty of determining, from the historical record of events preceding past wars, who was the aggressor. One side argues from that admitted and obvious difficulty that any attempt at a test would break down[1]; the other argues from the same facts that the invention of a new test is obviously necessary.

I believe there has been much too little recognition of the fact that in the nature of the case the outbreak of previous wars offers no close analogy to what would happen in a crisis in which the League was intervening. It is one of the incidental advantages of the procedure which the League normally does and should follow, when attempting to prevent a crisis developing to war, that if it fails it almost inevitably discloses incidentally the country which is at fault.

When there was a threat of war between Greece and Bulgaria, the Council met and devoted itself to arresting the drift to war. It did not in the first instance go into the question as to who was to blame for the original, probably trivial, incident which had caused the first firing of a rifle. Had war resulted, it would not have been on any judgment as to which was the culprit in this first incident that the League would

[1] Cf. Mr. Kellogg's Note of June 23, 1928, concerning the projected Pact of Paris. Referring to the "inalienable right" of self-defence and "the difficulty encountered in any effort to define aggression," the Note said (paragraph 1), "Inasmuch as no treaty provision can add to the natural right of self-defence, it is not in the interest of peace that a treaty should stipulate a juristic conception of self-defence, since it is far too easy for the unscrupulous to mould events to accord with an agreed definition." Sir Austen Chamberlain spoke in the same sense, likening any test of aggression to "a signpost for the guilty."—ED.

have pronounced guilt, or that its members would have determined against which country they should apply the sanctions of Article XVI, but upon the subsequent course of action. In order to prevent war, the Council required that under certain conditions and at certain times the Powers should withdraw their forces and observe certain rules of action. Had the Council's action been unsuccessful, it would have been the attitude of one of the countries towards such demands that would have shown which was really the aggressive country, and it would almost certainly have shown it in a way clear and indisputable beyond any analogy to be found in pre-League history where no such international action was possible. In such cases, too, the situation would be made more clear by the fact that the League would probably have its own agents on the spot during the period of danger.[1] This would again furnish evidence as to the fact of hostile action on one side or the other, for which there is normally no analogy in pre-League history.

It may be argued against this that cases could be

---

[1] Cf. The French Disarmament Plan, November 10, 1932. This provides for a special European organization of mutual assistance, to come into operation "when a territory under the authority of one of the signatory Powers is attacked or invaded by foreign forces." "The Council of the League of Nations will decide that assistance shall be given on simply ascertaining that an attack or invasion has taken place; in order to facilitate any steps that may be necessary to ascertain the facts, there shall be established in each of the signatory States a Commission consisting of diplomatic agents and military, naval, and air attachés. . . . Any State which believes itself to be threatened or alleges that it has been attacked may demand that the necessary measures be taken to establish the facts" (Chapter III, Section A).—ED.

both remembered and imagined in which the League's procedure would not disclose the aggressor in the way described above. On analysis, however, I think it will be found that the real defect in such cases consists in the political weakness of the League at the moment and in relation to the Powers involved and not in the absence of a test of aggression or the absence of reasonable certainty as to facts and their real nature. This is a difficulty therefore which, serious as it has been and may be, is really irrelevant to the question of the invention of a test of aggression.

In a word, in a war which follows the ineffective attempt of the League to handle a crisis, the culprit and aggressor will be not the country which, or whose national, was guilty of the original act out of which the crisis developed, but the country which, by refusing to follow the League recommendation adjusted to the original crisis, has caused the outbreak of war.

ARBITRATION

I hope that advantage may be taken of the prospects offered by the resolution of the Assembly to secure the draft of a model all-in arbitration treaty which could be used by pairs or groups of States prepared for such arbitration *inter se*.[1]

[1] The Protocol of 1924 would have been a multilateral treaty of pacific settlement for all kinds of international disputes between its signatories. When this was rejected, many States had recourse to bilateral treaties of pacific settlement In 1925 Sweden proposed that the League should prepare a model treaty: in 1927 the Labour and Socialist International approved a draft of an open treaty of all-inclusive pacific settlement prepared by the British Labour Party: and shortly afterwards Dr. Nansen submitted a similar draft (but omitting provisions for conciliation)

I have argued the general reasons for such an action in an earlier memorandum, and I need not repeat them here. I would only add that although to some extent such a treaty now comes perhaps "after the fair," other arbitration treaties are still likely to be arranged. Nor is it inconceivable that in some cases existing treaties might be transferred on to a new League model. Supposing, for example, that such pairs of treaties as those which have recently caused trouble between France and Italy should result in a difficult situation between two such countries; it is not inconceivable that negotiation between them might end by an agreement on both sides to arrange for substitution of League Model Treaties for those to which objection had been taken.

I think it is of vital importance that any such League model which is not universal in character but encourages treaties as between specially friendly countries should be limited absolutely to the provision for arbitration

before the Third Commission of the Eighth Assembly. His claim was that an "all-in arbitration" treaty, open for adhesion like the Optional Clause, would facilitate the spread of arbitration as fast and as far as the nations might be willing to go, under conditions which would avoid needless effort and diversity of texts, and would prevent conflict with the provisions or machinery of the League. The Eighth Assembly recommended "the progressive extension of arbitration by means of special or collective agreements" and decided that the Committee on Arbitration and Security should be set up, which "would first of all study every aspect of arbitration and more especially the concrete proposal which the Norwegian delegate has submitted to us." (M. Loudon, Rapporteur, September 28, 1927.) The Arbitration Committee produced three model treaties of arbitration and conciliation for use by pairs or groups of States: and the outcome was the "General Act" of September 1928.—ED.

inter se, without any provision or suggestion whatever of mutual aid in case of a conflict with a third party.

Of all the major, less immediate, causes of the Great War it is, I suppose, clear now that by much the most important was the development which resulted, about a quarter of a century ago, in the division of Europe into two rival armed camps. The experience of the last hundred years might be briefly summarized as follows:—

During the greater part of the nineteenth century there was a rapidly changing series of precarious alliances and understandings, in which the principle of the balance of power was important. Such a system was obviously difficult, dangerous, and anxious. But at least it had for the time some internal correctives and safeguards. A country developing aggressive strength or aggressive policy had to expect the alienation and possible hostility of "balancing" countries. And if war did break out, as in 1855, 1859, 1866, 1870, etc., it was possible for it to be more or less isolated; it did not necessarily involve all the Great Powers. But the difficulties, the constant anxieties and uncertainties of the system led, perhaps inevitably, to the new system (obviously foreshadowed in the last decades of the nineteenth century, but only completed in the first decade of the twentieth) of a more stable grouping of the main Powers into two sets of friends and potential foes.[1] Such a development presented some

[1] Cf. Lord Lansdowne's negotiation of the Entente Cordiale in 1904, and Sir E. Grey's authorization of military conversations with the French authorities in June, 1906. It is often assumed that British foreign policy continued until 1914 to be based on the principle of the "balance of power." It would be more true to say that that policy was ending in 1904.—ED.

obvious relief to harassed Foreign Ministers, feverishly watching for signs of new and possibly menacing alliances, secret or open, and haunted by the fear of their own country being isolated against a hostile world. But it meant that the correctives of the earlier, looser, system were gone, and probably that war, and a war involving at least all the great European Powers, was made inevitable—though not necessarily in 1914. For now that the grouping was more permanent in character, an increase in the military strength of a Power did not bring its former corrective in shifting political relations—it brought it in counter-preparations in the opposing group. An act of policy, with provocative possibilities, was no longer judged impartially and was no longer a factor as before in affecting political relationships. The process fatally led each year to increased armaments and less escapable commitments. The first increased the chances of war, the second prevented its limitation.

The League of Nations represented the exactly contrary conception of a completely universal and equal system, every Member State being equally responsible for settling difficulties and stopping war in any part of the world, no varying degrees of friendship or alienation or varying degrees of national interest in different regions being recognized.

For all who believe in the essential principles of the League, this must remain the ideal to which we must work: and for them any act of policy must be tested by the question whether it helps or hinders progress towards this end.

But the absence of America and Russia, and other

factors in the present world situation, prevent the application of the unqualified principle of "equal universality" to every measure. The experience and discussions of the last few years have shown what exceptions to this principle are desirable and innocent, and likely to assist progress towards the League's ultimate ideal, and what exceptions, on the contrary, are fundamentally inconsistent with it.

A few instances will suffice. After the "Triple Pact"[1] had lapsed through the absence of American ratification, the proposal of a British-French "unilateral" Pact against the danger of invasion by Germany was decisively condemned as inconsistent with the fundamental conception of the League.[2] On the other hand, the attempt to extend arbitration through the "universal" Protocol of 1924 has so far proved impracticable, some countries being unwilling to extend their "universal" obligations beyond those of the Covenant, though willing for extension within a more limited sphere.

[1] The Anglo-American Treaty of Guarantee to France in 1919. —ED.

[2] In January 1922, at a meeting of the Supreme Council, Mr. Lloyd George submitted to M. Briand a memorandum which, *inter alia*, offered France unconditionally an agreement by which Britain would undertake to assist France with all her forces in the event of unprovoked German aggression upon French territory. It was added that Britain would not accept such military commitments in Central and Eastern Europe. The Treaty was to be accompanied by an *entente*, to clear up all outstanding questions between the two countries. M. Briand replied that the guarantee must be not merely a British guarantee to France but reciprocal, and that it must be supplemented by a military convention. Briand resigned a few days later and the suggested Treaty of Guarantee eventually came to nothing.—ED.

The Locarno Agreements of 1925 were accepted as consistent with the League's fundamental conception because, though "regional" and not "universal," they were in no sense agreements of friends against States outside, but agreements on equal terms between countries recently at war, solely for the settlement of differences *inter se*.[1] Most important of all, the guarantee of the Franco-German frontier is in no degree unilateral; it applies equally either way. Any other principle would certainly have been regarded as inconsistent with the League conception. And I may add that the suspicion, whether just or not, that the Locarno Powers were later becoming a group for dealing with other questions than those *inter se* entitled to discuss collectively questions affecting other countries, was at once resented.

We may, I think, deduce from the experience and discussions of recent years that, where further development beyond the obligations of the Covenant is desirable, but is not practicable on a fully universal basis, regional or other limited engagements may be welcomed by the League in the following cases:—

(*a*) Agreements between pairs or groups of more closely associated, or more friendly, or geographically

---

[1] Cf. the British Government's observations on the programme of the Arbitration of Security Committee, January 1928. "The Treaty of Locarno is no mere alliance between a group of friendly States with a community of interests. Such alliances, unilateral in character and directed generally against some other State or group of States, have not always in the past best served the cause of peace. Even when originally inspired by defensive motives, they have sometimes become instruments of offence" (p. 53, C.A.S. 10, 1928).—ED.

contiguous Powers for arbitration of disputes *inter se*, which go beyond the provisions of the Covenant and also beyond what the countries in question would be prepared or able to agree to with all other countries.

But it is essential in such a case that there should be no provision, or suggestion, or encouragement, of the idea of the same Powers acting together in case of disputes or conflict with other Powers.

(*b*) Regional guarantees in addition to those of universal application under the Covenant.

But on the essential condition that the guarantees should, though regional, not be unilateral.[1]

Such arrangements (*a*) and (*b*) can therefore be properly recognized, endorsed, and indeed encouraged by the League.

At the other extreme, any treaty which provided for military aid under conditions inconsistent with and overriding the provisions of the Covenant should obviously not be concluded by any loyal Member, and might if concluded be properly objected to by other Members, who might in an extreme case hold that such action was inconsistent with continued membership of the League.

In between are a number of intermediate cases, viz.

---

[1] Cf. Observations of the German Government on the programme of the Arbitration and Security Committee, January 1928. Referring to regional agreements for collective security, Germany said:—"In every case, only such solutions should, of course, be sought as settle the relations between individual States belonging to a particular group without thereby bringing those States into opposition with States which do not belong to that group. An increase in the security of particular States at the expense of the security of other States constitutes no progress in the direction of peace" (C.A.S. 10, p. 59).—ED.

a Treaty formally consistent with and subject to the Covenant but such as to rouse doubt as to whether it would not result in the Covenant provisions being disregarded in crisis; one which indicates and confirms a political relationship likely to prevent an impartial attitude towards any dispute before the League in which one signatory might be involved with a third party; a treaty of military alliance which may be subject to the Covenant provisions but is "unilateral" and clearly contemplates military support to the Ally in the case in which the Covenant leaves a gap for private war and free judgment.

As to all these—varying as they do, or may, from the not quite harmless to the almost illegal and really dangerous—all one can say is that the League cannot formally stop them, but that Members, in proportion to their sincere loyalty to the League, are likely to avoid and discourage them.

I have developed this argument at some length because I believe that of all the tendencies which need careful watching in the interests of future peace there are none so serious as those which threaten a return to groups of friends and foes. Nor can there be, I think, a better criterion by which to judge whether League policy, and international policy in general, are developing in the right direction than the League's effect on political relationships of this kind. Is it tending to dissolve them and replace them by reliance on the more universal and impartial association of the League in Council and Assembly, or are such relationships tending to increase, under or in spite of League influence, as has been suggested by certain recent indications? No touchstone is, I believe, so sure a one as this—and none will be more required in the immediate future.

It is possible that the danger to which I have referred may be increased by an abuse of the last paragraph of the Assembly Resolution of September 26, 1927.

The Resolution says that the duty of the Arbitration and Security Committee would be "to consider . . . the measures capable of giving all States the guarantees of arbitration and security necessary to enable them to fix the level of their armaments at the lowest possible figures in an international disarmament agreement.

"The Assembly considers that these measures should be sought; . . .

in agreements which the States Members of the League may conclude among themselves, irrespective of their obligations under the Covenant, with a view to making their commitments proportionate to the degree of solidarity of a geographical or other nature existing between them and other States;

and further, in an invitation from the Council to the several States to inform it of the measures which they would be prepared to take, irrespective of their obligations under the Covenant, to support the Council's decisions or recommendations in the event of a conflict breaking out in a given region, each State indicating that, in a particular case, either all its forces, or a certain part of its military, naval, or air forces, could forthwith intervene in the conflict or support the Council's decisions or recommendations."

This paragraph doubtless contemplates the tabling of such an engagement as is taken in the Locarno Agree-

P

ments by Great Britain in defence of the frontier between Germany and France—an engagement which may be properly recognized and tabled by the League because, though regional, it is not "unilateral."

But there is an obvious danger that, in response to the Assembly invitation, some States may send in an offer to be tabled by the League, to supply such and such forces in case of aggression against A, or against A by B, without any corresponding offer in case of aggression *by* A against B or other countries. In such a case it seems to me that it would be disastrous for the League to receive and table such an offer. For such offers, made in response to a League invitation, could not be received and tabled without being recognized and encouraged. That is, the League, so far from discouraging and dissolving the system of grouping of friends against foes, would be encouraging and developing it.

But it will be difficult if a particular offer arrives before any attitude on principle has been taken. We should avoid the danger, if we could get a decision that it is the "Locarno" principle that the Resolution had in mind and that "unilateral" engagements should not be accepted and tabled.

It may be indeed that this particular danger may not develop. The whole of this part of the Resolution may prove a dead letter; or all States may, as regards a particular region, either make a "bilateral" offer or none at all.[1]

---

[1] This has proved to be substantially the case hitherto. The Arbitration and Security Committee drew up six Model Treaties. Three of these concerned arbitration and/or conciliation; the other three were a Collective Treaty of Mutual Assistance, a

Even so, such a decision would be an extremely useful opportunity of marking the true League attitude. For whether or not the paragraph in the Resolution quoted proves to be of importance, the main question discussed in the above pages is certain to be of vital and fundamental interest to the League in the immediate future.

Collective Treaty of Non-Agression, and a Bilateral Treaty of Non-aggression. At the time of writing (February 1933), the only one of these which has been used is the last, which was used by Greece and Roumania for their treaty in March 1928.—ED.

CHAPTER XIV

THE KELLOGG PACT

THE AMERICAN NOTE OF FEBRUARY 27, 1928

Editor's Foreword

THE American Note of February 27, 1928, to which this paper refers, was a turning-point in the history of the Kellogg Pact. On April 6, 1927, the tenth anniversary of the entry of the United States into the war, M. Briand, then Foreign Minister, had suggested a *bilateral* agreement between France and the United States for "renunciation of war as an instrument of national policy." On December 28, 1927, Mr. Kellogg proposed that the suggested Treaty, instead of being confined to the two Powers only, should be open to signature by all nations. The French Government made some difficulties about this; it suggested putting in a new formula renouncing "all war of aggression," and emphasized, in a far from cordial Note of January 21, 1928, that the new Treaty must not conflict with the existing obligations of League Members to participate in sanctions.

To this, Senator Borah, Chairman of the Foreign Relations Committee of the Senate, issued the open reply, quoted at the end of the paper, in an article on February 5th: and on February 27th Mr. Kellogg sent the Note to the French Ambassador which occasioned this paper.

Mr. Kellogg put the case for making the Treaty multilateral; recalled that at the recent Havana Conference of the American Republics seventeen Members of the League had passed a resolution condemning "war as an instrument of national policy"; and claimed that the Pact, instead of running counter to any obligations of the League, might be regarded as "a most effective instrument for promoting the great ideal of peace which the League has so closely at heart."

The French Government's reply of March 30, 1928, expressed willingness to join in sending a draft agreement, substantially the same as M. Briand's original proposal, to Britain, Germany, Italy, and Japan. Thereafter, the negotiations were directed towards a treaty open for adhesion by all States, such as the Kellogg Pact became.

THE KELLOGG PACT

I

THE AMERICAN NOTE OF FEBRUARY 27, 1928

(Written March 1, 1928)

The American Note published to-day seems to me, on any broad and long view, incomparably the most important fact in the present international position.

That a country with the actual and potential strength of the United States of America, at the moment when she has the power to embark upon the kind of imperialistic policy with which corresponding power by a single country has always hitherto been accompanied in the past, should take the lead in proposing a general treaty proscribing war as an instrument of national policy, may well mark a real epoch in history.

This must depend upon how it is received, and how it is followed up. The converse of the benefits which may follow if it is successful is the set-back that would follow failure. America may obviously, at this period of her history, turn towards an imperialistic and militaristic policy or to one of peaceful development. Her interests and her bodies of opinion are divided. The Government has given a definite lead towards the second; and if properly responded to, it may settle the issue. But if it is badly received, or unskilfully handled, it may have precisely the opposite effect; and the United States of America may turn towards a policy which would ultimately prove the greatest of all disasters to the rest of the world.

There is obviously, however, a real danger of the broader aspects and wider implications of the proposal being lost sight of, or inadequately assessed, because of minor and more technical preoccupations and short-range views.

A technical point may be quite sound, and may be made quite intelligible to those familiar with European considerations. But there is the greatest danger that it may be so presented as to give the impression in America that it is a pretext for general opposition.

Nor do I see that the technical difficulties in relation to the League are insuperable. The main question or adjustment is really met—or may be met—under the phrase "as an instrument of national policy"; and I cannot see why we on our side should create difficulties by asking whether this is meant to safeguard our Covenant obligations. Its natural meaning is that it does; and surely we should presume that it does—leaving to America the onus of insisting on a narrow meaning if she wants to, which I see no reason to believe.

As to the question of defence against invasion, surely this can be met without the use of the question-begging term "aggression" which is involved with all the Protocol controversies and necessarily evokes suspicion. Would it not be possible to accept as the basis of a treaty the proscription of war "as an instrument of national policy," i.e. otherwise than as means of

international enforcement of the observance of international engagements, and to add to the acceptance
something like this:—"In the drafting of the actual
text it would doubtless be desirable to include a
phrase which would make the Treaty clearly consistent
with the action which either the United States of
America or any other of the signatory States would
doubtless be compelled to take in the event of attack—
and we would ask the United States of America to
suggest the phrase." But the difficulty is perhaps less
in a multilateral than in a bilateral treaty, because, if
all countries come in, an act of aggression would
presumably mean breach of the treaty by the aggressor
and therefore the release of the other countries from
any restrictive provision of the treaty in relation to
that country (cf. Borah's "open letter").[1]

It is in my view a great mistake—it is playing the
game of anti-League and anti-pacific forces both in
the United States of America and elsewhere—to
speculate as to whether this is a "political move before
the election"; as to whether it "would mean much in
practice"; and as to whether it is "aimed at the
League."

For us it is the definite proposal of the responsible
Government of the United States of America. For us
it should mean what it says—and we should co-
operate to make it mean as much in practice. For us
it is an engagement extending the range of countries

[1] Senator Borah's article in the *New York Times*, February 5, 1928,
replying to the Note of the French Government of January 21st,
quoted on p. 234.—ED.

united for the ultimate objects of the League, though it does not mean that the engagements with and from America are as extensive as those between League Members; it is for us to see that they are not *inconsistent* with our own engagements between ourselves, and there is no reason why they should be.

It would clear away much understanding both in Europe and in America if a collective and authoritative pronouncement could make the real League position clear as regards such a proposal: viz. "We have certain engagements between ourselves; we cannot enter into new engagements with other countries which are inconsistent with these engagements. But that does not mean that we are unwilling to enter into engagements which, while not inconsistent with our existing engagements, are not co-extensive with them." The present proposal might well be such an engagement.

If the opportunity is not to be wasted—and perhaps worse than wasted—a collective reply or replies in identical terms from the Great Powers addressed by the United States of America are essential. And particularly as League interests are at the centre of the problem, it is natural that agreement should be attempted when the representatives meet at Geneva. There was a formal difficulty in seeing how the question could be discussed collectively on the basis of a correspondence between the United States of America and France. But the form of yesterday's letter, with the specific mention of France, Great Britain, Italy, Germany, and Japan by name, should remove this difficulty. The letter comes at precisely the right moment, and it would surely be a great disaster if next week were not used for the purpose.

From a League point of view, if we once have as a basis such a treaty as America proposes, we can rely on the logic of events to bring her nearer to the general League position.

Surely it is foolish to say—"What is the use of signing a Treaty not to go to war? You can't go to war without arranging a method of settling disputes; therefore let us not sign."

The right policy is surely "Let us sign the Treaty binding ourselves to achieve the end; having done that, the obligation will help—and impel—all of us to proceed to take all the further measures necessary for the purpose: that is, America will be brought step by step, by the same process as that which has moved countries which are nearer to the scene of immediate political troubles, to something like the League system.

ANNEX

EXTRACT FROM LETTER FROM SENATOR BORAH

(New York Times, FEBRUARY 5, 1928)

". . . As to France's other compacts or alliances, these are all supposed to be in harmony with the principles and provisions of the Covenant and to be filed with the League. Let us assume, for example, in the case of Belgium, which has been raised by the French, that France is absolutely obligated under her alliance to come to the relief of Belgium in case of attack. This commitment can be easily protected.

"All that is necessary is for the multilateral pact to be signed by Belgium, in which event all the signatories agree not to use war or force in any dispute or matter relating to Belgium. If an attack, nevertheless, is made on Belgium by one of the signatories it would constitute a breach of the multilateral treaty and would thereby *ipso facto* release France and enable her to fulfil her military engagements with Belgium. In other words, France's commitment to Belgium would merely be in suspense so long as the signatories kept their multilateral compact; there would be no violation thereof."

II

PROSPECTIVE BENEFITS AND DANGERS

(Written August 17, 1928, ten days before signature of the Pact)

POSSIBLE BENEFITS

The possible benefits of the Pact may be classed as follows :—

Moral Outlawry of War.—It gives a principle, clearly and intelligibly formulated, and accepted with full authority and ceremony by the great majority of nations, which may transform the general public attitude towards war. That is, it may substantially help public opinion to think of war instinctively and naturally as no longer one of the recognized institutions through which changes are effected or disputes settled, and to look upon armed forces as police forces.

This may ultimately be the most important effect. If secured, it would mean that all international engagements like the Covenant would be naturally applied in their strongest and fullest sense. This effect is weakened by interpretative reserves, so far, but only so far, as these remain in the memory of the public and alter their belief in the Pact.

Adverse criticism of the reserves, or depreciation of the Kellogg Pact because accompanied by reserves, increases the risk of this benefit being lost or reduced, unless it has the effect of removing the reserves themselves or getting them interpreted away or overridden.

Narrowing the Gap in the Covenant.—The Pact narrows somewhat, though in view of the reserves it can hardly be said to close completely, the gap in the Covenant (see below).

American Neutrality.—It is a foundation upon which full and adequate American responsibility for helping in securing the peace of the world may be built up; it should start the United States on the path leading to full and effective collaboration with the League.[1]

A war-making country, acting in breach of the League Covenant, will in future be breaking the Kellogg Pact also. This will mean that America must have a responsible view as to fault, etc. . . . As at the time the League Council will be the only body competent to be holding the necessary enquiry, America will naturally want to be associated with the League

[1] See Postscript.—ED.

in that enquiry. If sanctions should be required, active co-operation may follow.

At the least it should make interference by America in sanctions imposed by League members upon an aggressor impossible. And, what is equally important, it should prevent the aggressor from speculating hopefully upon the probable impotence of the Council caused by fears of American interference.

These benefits might well be so great as to make the Kellogg Pact much the most important event since the Covenant, not excepting Locarno. The reserves, however, make it impossible to estimate exactly the value which it is likely to have, and certainly there are some serious dangers.

POSSIBLE DANGERS

The principal dangers are the following :—

Rejection by Senate.—Rejection by the United States Senate is not impossible, though perhaps not probable.

Even if we take an extreme view as to the reduction of the value of the Kellogg Pact resulting from the reserves which have been made by various Governments, rejection by the Senate would be an immense disaster. It would stop for many years any effective association of America with European efforts to maintain peace, and would create a scepticism making any renewed attempt at a later date much more difficult. It would also give a kind of final effect and force to the reserves, as made in Europe and understood in their fullest sense.

The "British Monroe Doctrine" reserve and its phrasing, the tone and attitude of the French through the greater part of the negotiations, and more recently the extraordinary official publication of the fact that there is some kind of naval agreement with France, of which the terms are secret,[1] are factors increasing or creating this danger. A series of similar factors might make it a very grave one. Here again something may depend upon the character of public discussions of the Kellogg Pact and the reserves.

American Isolationism.—A considerable part of American opinion, conceivably enough to be decisive, may treat the Pact as rather the end, instead of the beginning, of American responsibility in relation to peace. They will say—"Now we can turn to getting on with the business that we are really concerned with—our economic development, etc. . . . As to the peace business, we settled that in 1928 by the Kellogg Pact." This may happen; but the organized opinion that wants closer and current association, and the logic of events themselves, together should rather secure the opposite result contemplated above.

Public Scepticism.—The reserves, their phrasing, their extreme range if given their fullest interpretation, and the tone of the accompanying statements generally, may result in the final public attitude towards the

[1] This refers to the Anglo-French naval compromise of 1928, in which the two Powers sought to clear the way for solution of some of the naval problems which had baffled the Preparatory Commission for the Disarmament Conference, and the Three-Power "Coolidge" Conference in 1927. The "compromise" was condemned by public opinion as soon as its terms became known in Great Britain, and sharply rejected by the United States.—Ed.

Kellogg Pact being as follows:—"The Governments have formally signed a document saying they renounce war; the accompanying statements show clearly that they do not mean to do any such thing. It is evident that this is one more piece of cant, and the new Treaty will not stop war any more than previous treaties; indeed no written statement can be relied on to change the position."

This might be the most serious evil effect, as the change in public opinion referred to above may possibly ultimately be the greatest benefit, of the Kellogg Pact, and this again constitutes one of the difficulties in public criticism.

Damage to the Covenant.—Apart from the general effect last mentioned of destroying public faith in all treaties, the reserves may have a destructive effect on the Covenant in being regarded as interpretations of the meaning of the Covenant itself, and indeed almost as interpretative amendments. In this respect their effect might be rather like that of the British statement of the reasons why the British Government would not accept the Protocol of 1924—reasons which in some cases seem to apply to the Covenant as well as to the Protocol. The provision in particular about self-defence—the statement made by Mr. Kellogg and adopted by both Great Britain and France that "each State alone is competent to decide when circumstances necessitate recourse to war for that purpose"— might certainly be very damaging.

This danger is discussed in more detail below. It is the one which gives the chief reason for public criticism and discussion now.

RESERVATIONS ABOUT THE PACT

A few notes may be added as to particular points in the reserves.

The "British Monroe Doctrine."—Paragraph 10 in the British Note of May 19, 1928, is as follows:—

> . . . "There are certain regions of the world the welfare and integrity of which constitute a special and vital interest for our peace and safety. His Majesty's Government have been at pains to make it clear in the past that interference with these regions cannot be suffered. Their protection against attack is to the British Empire a measure of self-defence. It must be clearly understood that His Majesty's Government in Great Britain accepts the new Treaty upon the distinct understanding that it does not prejudice their freedom of action in this respect. The Government of the United States have comparable interests any disregard of which by a foreign Power they have declared that they would regard as an unfriendly act. His Majesty's Government believe, therefore, that in defining their position they are expressing the intention and meaning of the United States Government."

To estimate the scope of this reserve it must be remembered that its object is to claim a right which would not otherwise remain on the signature of the Kellogg Pact, and to claim that right in spite of the definite understanding that no signatory will be bound as against any country which had already broken the Pact, and in spite of the understanding that we are still free to take action as Members of the League.

The "regions" are unspecified. It is not only their "integrity" but their "welfare" which is said to "constitute a special and vital interest for our peace and safety." "Interference with these regions cannot be suffered," and the new treaty "does not prejudice freedom of action in this respect," which would seem to imply that the Covenant does not already restrict freedom of action in the cases contemplated. This might, indeed, be true if the more restricted view of both the action and places is taken, but no such restriction or definition is included in the text.[1]

Lastly, the official reference to the interests of the United States (Monroe Doctrine) is regrettable, as it tends to arouse those particular forces and trends of opinion in America which all the wisest American friends of the Kellogg Pact particularly desired not to arouse.

Self-Defence.—Mr. Kellogg, in his speech to the American International Law Association on April 29, 1928, said: "There is nothing in the American draft of an anti-war treaty which restricts or impairs in any way the right of self-defence. That right is inherent in every sovereign State, and is implicit in every treaty. Every nation is free at all times and regardless of treaty provisions to defend its territory from attack or invasion, and it alone is competent to decide whether circumstances require recourse to war in self-defence. If it has a good case the world will applaud and not condemn its action."

[1] See Postscript.—ED.

The British Note of May 19th states that Sir Austen Chamberlain is entirely in accord with these views. The French Note repeats Mr. Kellogg's statement as an expression of its own views.

If this statement were understood in its fullest sense, it would seem to be destructive not only of the Kellogg Pact but of any loyal adhesion to the Covenant by the League Members who make it. Almost every country in modern times resorting to war has stated that it has done so in self-defence. Germany did so in marching through Belgium; Greece in invading Bulgaria in 1925 made the same plea.

This, however, is clearly to overstate the intention or probable effect of the reserve. As Mr. Kellogg says in the same passsage: "If it" (that is the country taking action in self-defence) "has a good case the world will applaud and not condemn its action." This means that the other signatories to the Pact in fact have to take their own view of the position. This incidentally forces them towards such an instrument of collective enquiry as the Council of the League.

Taking the whole passage of Mr. Kellogg's letter in relation to which the British and French statements were made and the emphasis on the maintenance of League obligations, it may perhaps be said that the real effect is, not to give a country a sole and final right to judge its own case and to exclude other countries from judging, but rather to safeguard a country, in signing the Kellogg Pact, from signing away any right it may retain under the Covenant to act *responsibly* without waiting first for a collective judgment. The country decides responsibly, subject to later appeal to judgment by other countries in the light of the principles of the Kellogg Pact and the Covenant. However, the position undeniably is left ambiguous and dangerous, and if possible any misapprehension should be removed (see below).

"*Rights and Obligations.*"—The words "rights and obligations" appear both in the French draft Treaty of April 21st[1] and in the Belgian acceptance of the Pact, dated July 18th. The French draft (Article IV) said: "The provisions of this Treaty in no wise affect the *rights and obligations* of the contracting parties resulting from prior international agreements to which they are parties." The Belgian acceptance "notes with satisfaction the interpretations of Mr. Kellogg, and observes with pleasure that the proposed treaty will maintain in their entirety the *rights and obligations* imposed by the Covenant of the League of Nations and by the Locarno Treaties which are fundamental guarantees of Belgium's security."

It is, of course, possible that the exception of "rights" might be interpreted in such a way as to prevent any narrowing of the "gap" in the Covenant that might otherwise result from the Kellogg Pact. I am, however, inclined to doubt this. The "right" to go to war which the gap in the Covenant allows in certain circumstances is not really a right *resulting from* the Covenant; it is a right that remains *in spite of* the Covenant's provisions, which have taken away the more extended right to make war that previously

[1] I.e. the draft Treaty submitted by the French Government to the Governments of United States, Britain, Germany, Italy, Japan, on April 20th, and published April 21, 1928.—ED.

existed. The rights which result from the Pact, particularly in a phrase which links together "rights and
obligations" in the same sentence, are surely rather
the rights which a country derives from the Pact
as a complement to its obligations, i.e. the right to
have the services of the League in settling its disputes
and the aid of its fellow-members in the circumstances
contemplated by the Covenant.

I should feel more doubt about this being a real
danger but for the fact that the phrase "rights and
obligations" does not appear in the last French reply,
but only in their proposed draft treaty; that the answer
given by Mr. Kellogg in substance deals only with the
"obligations" and does not in any way admit the "right
to war" left open by the gap in the Covenant apart
from the extent to which it is separately covered in the
self-defence passage; and that the final French Note
of July 16th accepts Mr. Kellogg's interpretation as
satisfactory, resuming it in the following words: "None
of the provisions of the new treaty is in opposition
either to the provisions of the Covenant of the League
of Nations or to those of the Treaties of Locarno or
of the Treaties of Neutrality. . . . In view of the
provisions of the preamble and the interpretations
given to the treaty, the French Government finds
that the new Convention is compatible with the
obligations of existing treaties to which France is a
contracting party."

It would be impossible to argue, I think, that anything in Mr. Kellogg's explanations admitted the
maintenance of the Covenant's "right to war" as
such. His argument is addressed solely to showing

that his Pact is not inconsistent with Covenant *obligations*.

DOES THE KELLOGG PACT CLOSE THE "GAP" IN THE COVENANT?

In principle the Covenant gap resulting from mere absence of agreement by the Council is closed.[1]

A League Member who has signed the Kellogg Pact and who takes warlike action against another signatory of the Pact must also claim that it is acting in self-defence, or in defence of one of the "Monroe" regions, or in execution of a (previously existing) treaty obligation or against a country which has already committed a breach. (I say *also* because the League obligations must be held to remain: e.g. a claim of self-defence must be subject to the same examination by the Council as at present.)

This is, however, a "gap within the gap," at best almost as wide as the original gap.

It is not easy to imagine the case in which a country, able without breach of the Covenant to resort to war, would regard itself as restrained from doing so solely by the extra *legal* obligation of the Kellogg Pact as interpreted by the reserves.

That does not conclude the matter, however. Such a country might well be restrained, first because, by the time the trouble arises, the world acceptance of the

---

[1] Cf. Article XV, paragraph 7. If a dispute likely to lead to a rupture is referred to the Council and the Council fails to reach a report upon it which is unanimous save for the votes of the disputants, then League Members recover an ultimate freedom to fight.—ED.

principle of the Pact may have changed the attitude of public opinion to a national war; and secondly because of the probable association of America with other countries against her in case of strained interpretation of the reserves.

The acceptance of the "principle" itself is much.

POSSIBLE ACTION

An Assembly Resolution.—Perhaps the most useful action, in view of the possible dangers, would be an Assembly Resolution.

This would need of course to be very carefully handled and worded, in view of possible reactions on the attitude of the Senate. But it might be possible.

It might include the following points:—

(i) A whole-hearted welcome might be given to the Pact, as making the "peace system" more comprehensive both by associating non-League States with the system and in narrowing the gap in the Covenant.

(ii) It might indicate that League membership, while of course preventing any new engagements involving reduction or weakening of existing reciprocal obligations of League Members *inter se*, does not prevent Members from contracting new obligations with other countries (including non-Members) which, while not inconsistent with, are not necessarily co-extensive with, League obligations. On the contrary, League Members welcome such agreements, as associating new States, as offering a supplement—not an alternative—to the League, and as basing the foundations of peace more broadly.

(iii) League Members who have signed the Kellogg

Pact might declare that they regard the Pact in the above light; that they remain loyal to the League's obligations in the fullest sense; that the explanations and reserves which have appeared in the correspondence connected with the Pact were intended solely as defining in certain respects the extent of certain *extra* restrictions which the Kellogg Pact might be thought to involve over the Covenant, not as in any way suggesting a limitation or interpretation of Covenant obligations; e.g. the statements as to self-defence are to be understood in the light of, and subject to, the League provisions and procedure.

(iv) An encouragement might also be offered to other League Members to sign the Kellogg Pact.

(The above of course is not an attempt at drafting—it merely suggests heads of possible contents.)

I do not know whether anything of the kind will be possible. But a skilfully worded resolution might be difficult to refuse.

POSTSCRIPT

BENEFITS

As regards the benefits anticipated, the Pact has undoubtedly had a considerable effect on public opinion, and has had some influence on the policies of Governments. Recall, for instance, the joint declaration of President Wilson and Mr. Ramsay MacDonald in October 1929, that "both our Governments resolve to accept the Peace Pact not only as a declaration of good intentions but as a positive obligation to direct national policy in accordance with its pledge." Note, also, the changed attitude towards war adopted by the Lambeth Conference of Protestant Churches in 1930; and the attitude of most of the spokesmen at the Special Assembly of the League, in March 1932, concerning the Sino-Japanese conflict.

Further, the Pact has had a manifest effect on the attitude of the United States as to collaboration in the prevention of war. In July 1929 the United States Government promptly consulted other signatories of the Pact in regard to a clash between China and the Soviet Union in Northern Manchuria. In July 1932 both the Republican and the Democratic Party Conventions at Chicago included in their platforms for the Presidential campaign proposals to make the Pact effective by provisions for consultation and conference in case of threatened violation of treaties: and Mr. Stimson, as Secretary of State, declared on August 8, 1932, that the Pact "necessarily carries with it the implication of consultation," and that the old doctrines of neutrality could not remain unaffected, war being now the concern of every nation and no longer the subject of rights. The principle of conference was also recognized by the United States, for certain purposes, in Article L of the Draft Disarmament Convention of 1930, and in the Resolutions of the Disarmament Conference on July 23, 1932. In the Sino-Japanese conflict, American collaboration was often close, and American policy often showed a clearer recognition of the principle of collective responsibility than that of some League Members. Indeed, in a Note of October 20, 1931, to Japan and China, the United States Government affirmed this principle explicitly, in terms which recall those of the first part of Article XI of the Covenant:— "The American Government, by representations through diplomatic channels, has steadily co-operated with the League in its efforts to secure a peaceful settlement. A threat of war, wherever it may arise, is of profound concern to the whole world, and for this reason the American Government, like other Governments, was constrained to call to the attention of both disputants the serious dangers involved in the present situation."

Amongst many evidences of such collaboration may be mentioned the official communication to the League of a Note sent by the American Government in January 1933 to the Peruvian Government in regard to a crisis between Peru and Colombia.

DANGERS

As regards the possible dangers foreseen in the paper, subsequent events have shown only too much justification for the apprehension expressed about the so-called "British Monroe Doctrine." So far as Great Britain herself is concerned, the reservation made by Sir Austen Chamberlain in May 1928 has had no traceable effect upon policy; and when the British adhesions to the Optional Clause and General Act (qualified though they are by large reservations) have been supplemented by the projected Amendments of the Covenant, and by a treaty of independence for Egypt, the reservation will have been largely sterilized so far as British "freedom of action" in unspecified regions is concerned. (Egypt and Persia, it may be added, expressly objected to the British "reservation," when they signed the Pact.)

But the British statement was important not only for its political effect on future British action but also as an encouragement to other States which might presently be tempted to claim "special and vital interest" in the "welfare and integrity" of territories not their own. An obvious example was Japan, with her great interests in Manchuria. Before signing the Pact, Japan proposed a Conference to discuss its principles; but this proposal was rejected, so Japan signed the Pact, and in doing so "was silent concerning any special reservations of its own."[1] But the danger was obvious from the outset that she might presently, with the British example before her, break down another huge gap in the Kellogg Pact by applying some sort of "Japanese Monroe Doctrine" to Manchuria. And when, a few years later, Japan did seize control of Manchuria, she did in fact defend her action on such grounds as Great Britain had indicated: she claimed freedom of action in "certain regions of the world," not Japanese, and she did so not on behalf of "the peace of nations" as conceived in Article XI of the Covenant but on behalf of "our peace and safety" as judged by Japan alone.

As a justification for this policy, the Japanese representative, M. Matsuoka, was able on November 22, 1932, to allude to the British "Monroe Doctrine" reservation to the Kellogg Pact.

AMENDMENT OF THE COVENANT

As regards the suggestion at the end of the paper—that the League should pass a Resolution declaring the new position created by the Pact in relation to the Covenant—the League chose another course. At the Ninth Assembly in 1928, the Lithuanian delegation proposed that the Council should examine the adaptation of the Covenant so as to bring it into line with the Pact. The Pact did not actually come into force till July 24, 1929: and the Lithuanian proposal was not then adopted. But at the Tenth Assembly Great Britain, supported by other Powers, made

[1] *War as an Instrument of National Policy*, by Professor Shotwell, 1929. Chapter on "Japan's Renunciation," p. 240.

a proposal to this effect, and then submitted a first draft of amendments; and the Assembly, in a Resolution, declared that "it is desirable that the terms of the Covenant of the League should not accord any longer to Members of the League a right to have recourse to war in cases in which the right has been renounced by the provisions of the Pact of Paris."

A committee of eleven then prepared amendments of the Covenant, but this proved a more difficult and far-reaching enterprise than had been anticipated. The Eleventh Assembly in 1930 failed to reach agreement on these draft amendments or on a redraft by another committee, and the issue was therefore postponed till 1931. But again in 1931, the Twelfth Assembly failed to reach agreement: and nothing was achieved in 1932. Thus the amendment of the Covenant, to harmonize it with the Pact, is still deferred: probably nothing definite will be done till the Disarmament Conference is within sight of conclusion or has ended.   ED.

CHAPTER XV

FOOD SHIPS

PRESIDENT HOOVER'S PROPOSAL FOR
IMMUNITY

Editor's Foreword

ON November 11, 1929, shortly before the London Naval
Conference began, President Hoover suggested in an
Armistice Day speech that food ships should be immune
from detention or capture in war-time and should be put
on the same footing as hospital ships.

The suggestion was not taken up.

Mr. Hoover's action was no doubt prompted to some
extent by his personal experience as Director of the Belgian
Relief Commission during the war, and as organizer of
the importations of food into Central Europe after the
Armistice. The widespread injury and suffering inflicted
by the great "hunger blockade" left a deep impression on
all who had experience of them: and Mr. Hoover, as a
member of the Supreme Economic Council in Paris in
1919, was in a unique position to receive full information
on the subject and to realize the tragic consequences of
the long shortage, followed by the long delay after the
Armistice before the first importations of food into Germany
were delivered.[1]

The President's proposal may be compared with the

[1] Under Mr. Hoover's direction, the amounts delivered between
March 25, 1919, the earliest date, until peace was signed on
June 28th, were 640,000 tons. The blockade was raised on
July 12th. By the end of August, when the original agreement
ended, the deliveries had reached 732,000 tons, apart from
imports from the Argentine, Scandinavia, and Holland.—ED.

Resolutions of the Second Assembly in 1921. In its nineteen "Resolutions concerning the Economic weapon," the Assembly said:—"14. In case of prolonged application of economic pressure, measures of increasing stringency may be taken. The cutting off of the food-supplies of the civil population of the defaulting State shall be regarded as an extremely drastic measure which shall only be applied if the other measures available are clearly inadequate."

The British Government (in a letter from the Secretary to the Cabinet to the Secretary-General, July 19, 1922) made the following comment:—"Resolution 14 suggests a distinction between civil and military populations. Such a distinction is hardly possible nowadays, and it is thought that the word 'civil' was perhaps included in the resolution by an oversight."

The President's proposed rule of war, on the other hand, included no distinction in favour of civil supplies: presumably the intention was that the rule should cover the food supplies for the armed forces as well as those for civilians.

FOOD SHIPS

PRESIDENT HOOVER'S PROPOSAL FOR IMMUNITY

November 1929

The proposals of President Hoover with regard to the free passage of food ships in case of war obviously call for serious and sympathetic consideration.

Mr. Hoover has indeed indicated that, at this stage, he is merely launching the idea privately and not officially, for free discussion by the public. He does not desire that the question should be discussed officially, at least until after the Naval Conference. The reasons for this—for avoiding all further complications for a conference already difficult—are overwhelming. It is assumed, therefore, that no official steps will be taken and no statement made of the British attitude by any member of the British Government until after the Naval Conference.

It is at the same time, however, clearly desirable that public opinion, which has been attracted to the subject by Mr. Hoover's speech, should from the first develop on lines which will help a successful conclusion to any official negotiations undertaken later; and also that the Government should prepare itself now to take a suitable attitude when the time arrives.

The following notes are written with a view to these immediate factors in the situation.

The proposal requires special attention to the following considerations :—

There is a serious disadvantage, at a time when the world's principal attention is directed, and needs to be directed, to making a future war impossible, in diverting it to the question of the rules to govern the conduct of such a war. It tends to give unreality to the engagements to refrain from war, and to reduce the general confidence in their observance, upon which their validity depends. More important, it tends to delude the public into believing that war can be to a tolerable degree "humanized." It tends, therefore, to reduce the feeling that it is a criminal and disreputable thing; and by consequence to reduce the forces that now collectively support the efforts to prevent war. It would have been an unwise thing for any Government which in the past was attempting to end the practice of duelling to deal at the same time with the enforcement of rules as to the conduct of duels. Duelling was suppressed by treating it as murder. War will be suppressed by treating the offender as a criminal with only the rights of an outlaw.

There is a further danger in the fact that the proposal, in the form in which it has been put forward, tends to obscure the vital distinction between the criminal war upon which a country has embarked in breach of the Kellogg Pact and the Covenant, and the "police action" necessitated on the part of other countries by the outbreak of such a war.

The revision of international law which will in due course be required to make it conform with the situation created by the Pact and Covenant will doubtless make this distinction the basis of its provisions; and it is similarly taken as fundamental in the following notes.

Let us first take the proposal as regards the rights of a belligerent who has wrongfully resorted to war. For this it appears both inadequate and ineffective. Certainly it would be easy to agree, in revising international law, that such a wrongful belligerent should not have a recognized right to interfere with the passage of food ships to the victim of his aggression or to anyone else. But surely, in such a revision, his rights should be restricted much more than that. The conception of "outlawry" would indeed seem to imply that he should have *no* rights.

The proposal would also, by itself, be ineffective as a restraint upon such a wrongful belligerent. For if, to *begin* a war, he has been ready to break his engagements under Pact and Covenant, it is not to be expected that when actually fighting he will handicap himself in order to comply with another treaty.

Common sense suggests, and experience confirms, that a treaty engagement may restrain a country from breaking the peace, but that once a country is fighting for its life it will not be restrained by treaty from doing anything which it regards as vital to its success. Certain Red Cross and White Flag provisions owe their observance, in so far as they are observed, to the fact that they do not represent a crucial factor in victory or defeat. Renunciation of the use of gas, or the immunity of food ships, will be a fragile chain for the guilty—and a trap for the innocent.

For a provision that will not restrain a country

which has already broken its engagements to begin war may both delude other countries and make them impotent to deal with the aggression and the methods which accompany it. Let us consider the proposal as affecting the belligerent rights of countries interested in, or pledged to secure, the observance of the Kellogg Pact and Covenant, when they are dealing with the situation created by an illegal resort to war by another country.

A prior and general engagement not to interfere with food ships destined to the aggressor country presents the following difficulties :—

(*a*) Not only is food for civilians not distinguishable from food for the military forces; but food itself is often not distinguishable from the raw materials for munitions. Barley and oil seeds are two among numerous examples.

(*b*) An undertaking to give passage to food ships practically implies the principle that the "police action" of the community will not be such as to cause starvation. And this affects much more than food ships. The stoppage of food ships to Germany was a much smaller factor in her starvation than the stoppage of fodder and fertilizers. Moreover, if a country cannot pay she cannot import. And thus a stoppage of her general trade might well in time cause starvation. It was a stoppage of copper, not of corn, which caused bread riots in Leghorn in 1915, and shortage of cotton which caused starvation in Lancashire in the American Civil War.

Once, therefore, Mr. Hoover's proposal had been accepted—and all the forces to which it appeals mobi-

lized behind it—extensions would probably be gradually pressed for which would ultimately deprive loyal
signatories of the Pact and Covenant of any right of
effective blockade against a guilty belligerent.

(d) Where the wrongful belligerent is a food-
exporter, the free passage for his ships (which is a part
of the proposal) would maintain his financial resources
by payments from the nationals of the States whose
major interest is to stop the peace-breaking as rapidly
as possible.

The acceptance of the principle might therefore
result in the "police action" countries being entirely
impotent to stop an illegal war—except by resorting to
military or naval force. With either inaction or military
or naval action the toll in human suffering would
probably be much greater than that involved in a
sharp, and probably short, exercise of the full blockade,
with its irresistible demonstration (otherwise impossible) of the world community's determination to end
the war.

Nevertheless, League Members will doubtless sym-
pathize sincerely with Mr. Hoover's proposals to the
extent of wishing, in taking action under Article XVI,
to do so in such a way as to cause the minimum of
human suffering—always remembering, however, to
take into account the extra suffering involved by the
continuance of the war for a longer period if their
action is rendered impotent.

They will be the more anxious to go as far as possible
to meet Mr. Hoover because they recognize, as he
does, that in spite of the extent (still limited) to which
Governments are based upon representative institu-

tions, the guilt is the guilt of the Government, not that of the masses of civilians who have been taken by them into the illegal war.

With these considerations in mind the following might be a practical proposal:—

League Members, who have a definite right under existing international law and a definite duty under Article XVI to impose a complete blockade, including the stoppage of food ships, against a wrongful belligerent, might agree to modify both their rights and their duties by a general treaty entered into beforehand.

This treaty could provide that an *exception would be made in any blockade measures undertaken against the aggressor, to the extent necessary to permit any relief decided to be practicable, in the circumstances of the particular case, to the population of the aggressor country, by a conference of the signatories to the Kellogg Pact and the Covenant.* This might take the form either of permitting the passage of certain classes and numbers of ships, or of directly providing and convoying relief ships under a system similar to that of the Belgian Relief Commission.

At such a conference the convenience of effective consultation and the need for rapidity of action would probably lead to the League Members being represented through the Council, which would in any case be meeting to deal with the general situation. It would not be difficult to arrange for the necessary conference, for this purpose if for no others, between the League Members so represented and other signatories of the Kellogg Pact.

Such an arrangement—and apparently only such an

arrangement—would secure the greatest possible restriction of human suffering resulting from police action compatible with the avoidance of much greater human suffering which would result from the continuance of the illegal war.

Suggested form of statement by an individual Government:—

"We would be glad to undertake that, if resort to war is threatened or committed in breach of the Kellogg Pact or Covenant, we will confer with League Members (by means of the Council) and with those signatories of the Kellogg Pact who are not Members of the League; and we undertake to allow free passage of food (whether civil or military supplies, State or private property), in such measure as may be deemed advisable by such a conference."

NOTE AS TO REASONS UNDERLYING FOREGOING PROPOSAL

Mr. Hoover's proposals were to a large extent based upon a misinterpretation of the real position as regards sanctions under the Covenant. He says, "the European nations [sic] have, by the Covenant of the League of Nations, agreed that if nations fail to settle their differences peaceably, then force should be applied by other nations to compel them to be reasonable. We have refused to travel this road." This states incorrectly what the Covenant really does and ignores the problem with which it seeks to deal. The sanctions of Article XVI only apply to a case where a State has actually *resorted to war* in breach of the Covenant. There is no provision for the use of force to compel nations to be "reasonable" if they "fail to settle their differences peaceably." President Hoover ignores the unescapable problem—What is to be done to put a stop to a breach of the common peace if it should happen?

The proposal in my note fully recognizes the distinction so strongly felt in America between the guilt of the Government and the civilian population.

It is obviously constructed to meet Mr. Hoover's fundamental desire, that is, to reduce the amount of human suffering involved in a particular world crisis to the absolute minimum; and to the extent to which it does not fully accept his proposal it shows that the only reason is that the result of full acceptance would actually involve greater human suffering.

It would promote the idea of conference between League Members and non-Members, in the event of war or threat of war, thereby facilitating the use of Pact and Covenant for prevention purposes, and reducing the danger that sanctions may have to be used.

This consideration is the more important because the arrangement would be one growing out of Mr. Hoover's own proposals; because it would not only, in fact, require conference when the crisis arose, but would involve a prior arrangement with America contemplating such a conference. Precedents for this already exist in the Pacific Agreement, and in the provisions in regard to the Permanent Court of International Justice. This is also along the line on which Mr. Hoover's own mind is clearly working, as is shown by his Armistice speech.

It may be added that it also has the advantage of being entirely in accord with the line of the present British Government's policy.

CHAPTER XVI

FREEDOM OF THE SEAS

Editor's Foreword

THIS paper was written shortly before the Naval Disarmament Conference began (January 1930), and at a time when the question of "Freedom of the Seas" was being much discussed, both in England and in America.

Two conceptions of "Freedom of the Seas" were involved. On the one hand there was the old "Freedom of the Seas," which stood for certain compromises between the claims of neutrals and belligerents in a legitimate private war; e.g. the doctrine that "private property at sea, excepting contraband, should be immune from capture," and the doctrine, "free ships make free goods." It was apparently in accordance with this traditional conception that Senator Borah was urging throughout 1929 that the Naval Disarmament Conference should be preceded and prepared for by a conference on Freedom of the Seas; he laid special emphasis on the immunity of private property at sea from capture.

On the other hand, there was the modern doctrine of Freedom of the Seas, formulated by President Wilson in the second of his Fourteen Points: "absolute freedom of navigation upon the seas, outside territorial waters, alike in peace and in war, except as the seas may be closed in whole or in part by international action for the enforcement of international covenants." During 1929 this conception received growing recognition in the United States and especially in England.

The important resolutions introduced into the Senate and House of Representatives by Senator Capper and

Representative Porter on February 11, 1929, may be counted as steps in this direction.

Both in the United States and in Great Britain there were many publications on this subject. In England, for instance, there was a pamphlet by the Labour Party, with a preface by Mr. Ramsay MacDonald, issued during the General Election before the party came into office and declaring that "the Labour Party stands for the complete renunciation of the right of private war and private blockade. We stand for the full acceptance of the new doctrine of Freedom of Seas, i.e. that the high seas should *only* be closed by international agreement for the enforcement of international covenants. We stand for loyal and effective co-operation in the League's sanctions against a State which resorts to war in breach of its covenant."

Nothing was decided about Freedom of the Seas at the London Naval Conference. But on December 12, 1929 (just after the present paper was written), the British Government issued a statement of its reasons for signing the Optional Clause which had an important bearing on the subject. The Covenant and Pact, it said, had together brought about "a fundamental change in the whole question of belligerent and neutral rights"; and it expressed the view that "as between Members of the League there can be no neutral rights, because there can be no neutrals." On January 27, 1930, the Foreign Secretary, Mr. Henderson, declared that, thanks to the Kellogg Pact, the only war in which the British fleet could be engaged in future would be a war arising out of the terms of the Covenant. That implied that the Government regarded itself as committed to "complete renunciation of the right of private war and private blockade." It was to this end also that the proposed amendments of the Covenant, not yet adopted, were directed.

FREEDOM OF THE SEAS

December 5, 1929

GENERAL OBSERVATIONS

The following are the main factors in the position:—

(a) In the last war the geographical position of Germany and the submarine together rendered close blockade impracticable. Therefore, without the application of the continuous blockade principle, the blockade would have been ineffective.[1]

(b) The experience of that war showed also the unreality, and, to a large extent, the impracticability of distinctions between either contraband and non-contraband articles or between private and public property. In a war of peoples of which the whole

---

[1] The weapon of "close blockade" could never be applied by Great Britain throughout the war, except in the Red Sea and a small area at Zanzibar. For the rest, the entire "blockade" was effected by a long-distance cordon, which included neutral ports within its area; and the weapon which Britain had to rely on was the right to capture contraband, even though consigned to a neutral port. At The Hague Conference in 1907, and in the Declaration of London in 1909, British policy had been based on the opposite assumption; the Admiralty at that time were content to see the rules of contraband drastically curtailed or even abandoned, so long as the power of "effective blockade" was retained. And yet, when the war came only five years later, it was found useless even to declare a "blockade" of Germany, such as the Declaration contemplated: and Britain, who had not yet ratified the Declaration, promptly set about resharpening the weapons of contraband which she had lately gone far to destroy. Cf. the Order in Council of August 20, 1914, adopting the Declaration but reversing its cardinal principle.—ED.

economic resources and the whole populations are engaged, both distinctions cease to have much meaning.[1]

[1] This was clearly brought out in the *Wilhelmina* case in January 1925. This ship was detained by the British naval patrols, having a cargo of foodstuffs consigned to Hamburg for the use of the civil population. The cargo was accompanied by a guarantee that it would only be sold "to the populace or private purchasers of Germany, and not to any belligerent Government or to any agent thereof, or to military or naval forces, or any contractor or agent supplying military forces." According to the Declaration of London, the cargo would have been liable to seizure if destined for the use of a "Government Department of the Enemy State" (Article XXXIII), but immune if destined for a Municipality (Report on Article XXXIII). It would have been liable to seizure if destined for the armed forces (Article XXXIII), but not if destined for the civilian munition workers. It would have been liable to seizure if consigned to "enemy authorities or a contractor established in the enemy country who as a matter of common knowledge supplies articles of this kind to the enemy" (Article XXXIV), but immune if consigned to private individuals other than "agents of the enemy State" (Order in Council of October 29, 1914). All these distinctions had of course been observed by the guarantors of the *Wilhelmina*'s cargo. There remained, however, one point against which they did not guard. Hamburg could be treated as a "base for the armed forces of the enemy." It was on this ground that the *Wilhelmina* and her cargo were detained for Prize Court proceedings; but for political reasons they were at once released for sale to the Belgian Relief Commission.

Manifestly in such a case, in a war between organized modern States, all these theoretic distinctions had ceased to be real. Even if every ton of food imported into Hamburg "for the civilian population" had been consumed by civilians, its importation would have served to release an equivalent supply for the soldier in the field: and the State, naturally and rightly, was concerned to maintain the supplies of both. As Sir E. Grey said in his Note to the American Government about this cargo on February 10, 1915, "The reason for drawing a distinction between foodstuffs intended for the civil population and those for the armed forces or enemy Government disappears when the distinction between

(c) It is this experience, and in particular the memory that, had the Declaration of London been ratified and observed, the blockade against Germany would have been largely paralysed, that mainly explains the British attitude since the war.

These, however, are the old factors. British opinion has not taken into account the new factors in the situation. The principal of these are: (a) We were able to apply our system against the protest of America because in 1915–16 America still had a weak Navy. This situation is very unlikely to be repeated. It is scarcely possible to conceive the position in which Great Britain would both decide on military grounds to impose the same kind of blockade as in the last war, and would be able to, against the American opposition, in view of the present and future American strength. (b) The situation has, moreover, been greatly changed by the provisions of the Covenant and the Kellogg

the civil population and the armed forces itself disappears. In any country in which there exists such a tremendous organization for war as now obtains in Germany, there is no clear division between those whom the Government is responsible for feeding and those whom it is not."

It may be added that the German authorities came to a similar conclusion. As early as September 1914 a neutral ship, the Dutch s.s. *Maria*, with a cargo of grain shipped from a neutral port before the outbreak of war, consigned to Dublin and Belfast and sold in the ordinary course of business to British merchants, was sunk by the German cruiser *Karlsruhe*: and the German Prize Courts judged that the ship and cargo were liable to condemnation on the ground that there was no certainty that the British Government might not have bought the wheat or the flour made from it! As General Ludendorff wrote: "In this war it was impossible to distinguish where the sphere of the army and navy began and that of the people ended. Army and people were one" (*My War Memories*, Vol. I, p. 2).—ED.

Pact, which aim at the abolition of most private wars, while the provisions of the Covenant at least constitute a definite distinction between private wars and public "wars."

It will be well to consider the two cases separately.

PRIVATE WARS

If we consider the position as it would have been without any Covenant or Kellogg Pact, and purely as a matter of policy framed with a view to wars of the pre-war type, the following observations seem pertinent.

For the reasons stated above, it is scarcely possible to conceive the case in which Great Britain would want to use, and be able to use, the blockade in a form which is inconsistent with the American theory. It would therefore be giving up nothing of value to abandon the British theory.

If Great Britain were a neutral, the prior experience of American theory would be of great advantage. If, for example, the United States were at war with Chili, the British "continuous voyage" theory, which shut the whole of South America, would deprive Great Britain of the whole of her South American trade. (It is one of the interesting features of the controversy that America always imagines herself as a neutral and Great Britain always as a belligerent.)

More important, the full freedom of the seas principle, if accepted generally and in particular by the United States and Great Britain, would constitute the best safeguard possible against Great Britain's one vital danger, namely, the stoppage of her imports.

Indeed, American underwriting of such a principle might have developed into a safeguard for England comparable to the British guarantee of France's Eastern frontier at Locarno. It is difficult to conceive an object of British foreign policy so valuable, and it is curious that Great Britain at Paris made it a first object not to secure but to destroy such a principle. The actual explanation was, of course, the recent experience and the considerations indicated in the first part of this note.

Therefore, in so far as we are considering private wars, it would probably be to the very great advantage of Great Britain to be ready to accept the freedom of the seas principle, both for the above reasons, and also because it would facilitate generally good relations with America.

PUBLIC WARS

The Covenant, however, makes all wars, except those which slip through the "gap," illegal; and against those who make such illegal wars, economic and financial blockade is the principal sanction. The Kellogg Pact legally narrows the League gap—that is, makes illegal most of even those wars which are legal under the Covenant.

In these circumstances, it would be desirable if possible to make an absolute distinction between what is permitted by a private belligerent and what is permitted by States acting together against an aggressor who makes war in breach of the Covenant or the Kellogg Pact, the blockade rights of the belligerent being restricted to the narrowest American doctrine for the first, and if practicable no restrictions being imposed for the second. It would, of course, be best if America could be induced to agree not to insist upon a neutral's rights to interfere with action taken by the League, or in relation with the Kellogg Pact, against an aggressor.

It is, however, to be expected that America would not accept the verdict of League Members alone; but it would be sufficient if she would agree not to insist on neutral rights, in a case in which *she herself* was convinced that the blockade undertaken was genuinely undertaken as a police measure against an aggressor. In fact, this would only put her in the same position as League Members, each of which retains its right of separate judgment as to whether the conditions requiring the application of the sanctions of Article XVI have arisen or not. The difficult problem which may arise is, what line should be taken if America refuses to make any distinction between private and public wars, and presses for the complete freedom of the seas principle in both cases.

The above statement shows the reasons why a detailed study of all the aspects of the freedom of the seas problem is much needed. Among these is a legal study of the legal effects in international law of the Kellogg Pact.

The matter is of course of special importance because, apart from its intrinsic interest, it may be the way back both to good understanding with America and in particular to the settlement of the naval problem. It may be that discussion on freedom of the seas at a conference, such as that which has been suggested by Borah and Lee, ought to precede a renewed attempt to arrange or define parity in cruisers; but it is essential that, before this is done, any Government undertaking it should have studied the question in all its aspects, and if it decides upon a new policy it should have done something to educate British public opinion.

CHAPTER XVII

NOTES ON SECURITY AND CONFIDENCE

Editor's Foreword

THE following note was written in June 1931, when the author had just returned from a visit to the Far East and the United States, which concluded his service with the League Secretariat.

It expressed his opinion, based upon personal contacts in America, as to the lines upon which a development of co-operation between America and League Members would be most practicable and most useful. The note was given to personal friends on both sides of the Atlantic and the views expressed were developed further in the author's book *Recovery: The Second Effort*, published in April 1932.

The conflict between China and Japan, which began in September 1931 and still continues, has resulted in the development, in practice, of a procedure of regular consultation between America and the League; and the classic speech of Mr. Stimson, the Secretary of State, to the Council of Foreign Relations, on August 8th makes a corresponding development in doctrine and permanent principles of policy. He there develops the argument that the Kellogg Pact, by rendering war illegal, has made neutrality obsolete; that that Pact is not a mere collection of unilateral statements by the signatories, but a treaty conferring rights and liabilities; and that consultation between the signatories of the Pact when faced with the threat of its violation becomes inevitable.

The memorandum submitted by Mr. Stimson to the House Foreign Affairs Committee, towards the conclusion of his term of office as Secretary of State, marks a further development of doctrine. This memorandum, which was in support of a Resolution to authorize the President to join other countries in a refusal to allow the shipment of arms whenever the shipment would promote war, includes the following notable passage :—

"In the case of a war between two foreign countries the embargo would not, of course, be employed unless there was general co-operation and united opinion among the principal world Powers who could supply munitions. If there was no developed public opinion or international attitude, it is obvious that the employment of the measure by this country would be fruitless and improper. If there was public opinion and general world concern leading to co-operation, one of two conditions would exist—(a) the world would co-operate in refusing supplies to both nations; this would certainly involve no breach of neutrality by the United States as the movement would be general and the nations united in a common front; (b) there might be a situation in which as a result of investigation and consultation on a large scale there was a clear definition agreed upon by all the co-operating Powers that one side or the other was the aggressor.

"It is becoming evident in recent years that this condition is much easier to realize than used to be believed. The world-wide publicity afforded since the Great War on every international incident and army movement and the means of investigation by international commissions which is rapidly gaining ground, all show that there are situations to-day in which there can be a general verdict far beyond previous anticipation. The verdict of the League of Nations on this subject, for example, as shown by recent events, is a perfectly practicable procedure. If the League or any other comprehensive group of important States had mutually arrived at such a verdict, the participation of the United States in a general arms embargo would be not merely practical and sound, but practically necessary to preserve our national dignity and standing as a peaceful nation."

NOTES ON SECURITY AND CONFIDENCE

JULY 1931

The most important adverse factor in regard to disarmament, and one of the two most important factors in the whole of the financial and economic trouble, is the absence of confidence as to the maintenance of peaceful relations, particularly between European countries.

This want of confidence is caused partly by a series of well-known disputes and grievances. The fundamental cause is, however, not this, but a doubt as to whether the "universal" or "collective" principle which is embodied alike in the Covenant of the League, the Kellogg Pact, and the Locarno Treaty, will prevail over the alternative policy of each country relying on its own military strength, or its own strength fortified by military alliances. These two principles are now visibly competing for the mastery of the world's fate. Neither will in any near future completely oust the other. Covenant and Kellogg Pact, on the one hand, and national armaments and alliances on the other, will both continue as factors in the world's policy. But if year by year the first becomes more and more the real and recognized basis of each nation's security, and the effective basis of its policy, peace will be assured. If year by year the movement is in the other direction; if armaments grow; if alliances harden and strengthen; if the actual power of Covenant and Kellogg Pact seem more shadowy and speculative, war will ultimately be inevitable, whatever the moment or occasion.

The great need, therefore, is to strengthen the "collective" system.

It is not enough that, in fact, this system should work when the issue of war and peace occurs. It is essential that beforehand and at once people should have confidence that it will be effective; for the immediate danger is not a danger of war, but a danger that countries will now and increasingly, through lack of confidence in the efficacy of the universal system, base their current policy on national armaments and military alliances. In that case a restoration of confidence is impossible, and in that event *inter alia* the financial crisis cannot be solved, and the Disarmament Conference is doomed to failure.

How then can the "collective" system be strengthened?

Great Britain can at this moment do little, if anything, more, for two reasons:—

(*a*) In the first place, there is a strong feeling amongst the British public that if anything Great Britain has gone too far without America in under-pinning the "collective" system. She has continued to pledge herself to the onerous obligations of Article XVI of the Covenant, although when she originally accepted this she did so in the expectation that America would also be associated. She has, in addition, played her last card in promising to throw in the whole of her military and naval forces against France if France should attack Germany across the Rhine Frontier, or against Germany if Germany should attack France across the same frontier.

(*b*) The second reason is that no extra engagements by Great Britain would be effective in giving confidence in the "collective" system in Europe, because the real doubt in Europe is as to whether Great Britain would, in fact, be able to stand by her existing engagements if America's attitude were adverse.

The restoration of political confidence, therefore, depends upon whether America can follow up her financial lead[1] by a political lead.

What could America do?

Well, first, what is it impossible for her to do?

I take it that in view of the deep-rooted traditions of American opinion and policy, she cannot do any one of the following things in any near future :—

(*a*) She cannot ratify the Covenant or accept its political engagements.

(*b*) She cannot constitutionally or politically accept an engagement which would bind her in a future crisis to forego her ultimate right of independent judgment, or accept the verdict of other countries.

(*c*) She cannot undertake beforehand to take an active part in any circumstances in a blockade.

But, without doing any of these things, she could, I suggest,

(*a*) Declare that the principle of the Kellogg Pact (not to use war as an instrument of national policy) is not only one which will determine her own policy, but is the principle by which she will determine her attitude towards the action of other signatories. (This means that in case of a Kellogg Pact signatory resorting to war, America would be free to judge which was to blame,

[1] I.e. the Hoover Moratorium of June 1931.

but she would be pledged to judge with reference to the principle of the Kellogg Pact. She would not be free to say "country A is my friend, and I stick to her, right or wrong." She would be pledged to judge which was wrong. She would not, however, be bound as to what course of action should follow from such a judgment.)

(b) She might state now her willingness in the case of actual or threatened resort to war by a Kellogg Pact signatory, to consult other signatories in such a way as not to replace or weaken, but to supplement the machinery of the League for League Members. This would leave her free to make her own ultimate decision herself, but the decision would be taken after consultation and therefore with full knowledge of the facts, and not without it. This might take the form of a proposal to other Kellogg Pact signatories to sign an additional undertaking to consult together, or it might be a unilateral statement of willingness on America's part. A statement of such willingness was nearly made at the time of the Naval Conference; it was then dropped mainly because, if inserted as an item in a Naval Disarmament Treaty, it seemed impossible to avoid giving it implications which went beyond what America was willing to allow. This difficulty does not arise if the action were taken, if the announcement were made, independently of an actual disarmament negotiation. In effect, such an announcement has, I believe, been made by Mr. Gibson at one of the disarmament meetings, but an announcement made in that form is not sufficient; it needs to be made directly as a Presidential announcement, and in conjunction with such other proposals as are here suggested.

(*c*) An announcement could, I suggest, further be made that America would not recognize any country which America herself regards as having resorted to war in breach of the Kellogg Pact as having any of a pre-war belligerent's rights.

(*d*) An announcement might also be made that if America, in the exercise of her own judgment, considers that a Kellogg Pact signatory is resorting to war in breach of that Pact, and that any action taken by League Members under Article XVI is in America's own judgment designed solely to stop that illegal action, America will at least do nothing to interfere. She will not act so as to give aid or succour to a country which she herself recognizes to be unlawfully belligerent. This would leave her judgment free, and also leave her free as to whether she took any positive action.

I suggest that there is nothing in these four announcements which would be counter to the fundamental traditions of American policy, and that, if made in the form of a Presidential declaration they might well be accepted and embodied in American traditions as the Monroe Doctrine itself was.

There can be no question whatever that such an announcement of America's intention (in effect, to leave the Wilson Pact intact, and make the Kellogg Pact effective), would be a contribution of the utmost, and probably of decisive, importance in restoring political confidence, and making the "collective" system the basis of policy throughout the world.

It is evident that the world situation cannot wait long. Such an announcement made before the end of this year might be of decisive importance, whereas a month or two later the financial collapse may have come, and the situation may have drifted to a point at which it would be no longer effective.

APPENDIX

THE COVENANT OF THE LEAGUE OF NATIONS

THE HIGH CONTRACTING PARTIES,

In order to promote international co-operation and to achieve international peace and security

> by the acceptance of obligations not to resort to war,
> by the prescription of open, just, and honourable relations between nations,
> by the firm establishment of the understandings of international law as the actual rule of conduct among Governments,
> and by the maintenance of justice and a scrupulous respect for all treaty obligations.in the dealings of organized peoples with one another,

Agree to this Covenant of the League of Nations.

ARTICLE I

1. The original Members of the League of Nations shall be those of the Signatories which are named in the Annex to this Covenant and also such of those other States named in the Annex as shall accede without reservation to this Covenant. Such accession shall be effected by a Declaration deposited with the Secretariat within two months of the coming into force of the Covenant. Notice thereof shall be sent to all other Members of the League.

2. Any fully self-governing State, Dominion, or Colony not named in the Annex may become a Member of the League if its admission is agreed to by two-thirds of the Assembly, provided that it shall give effective guarantees of its sincere intention to observe its international obligations, and shall accept such regulations as may be prescribed by the League in regard to its military, naval, and air forces and armaments.

3. Any Member of the League may, after two years'

notice of its intention so to do, withdraw from the League, provided that all its international obligations and all its obligations under this Covenant shall have been fulfilled at the time of its withdrawal.

ARTICLE II

The action of the League under this Covenant shall be effected through the instrumentality of an Assembly and of a Council, with a permanent Secretariat.

ARTICLE III

1. The Assembly shall consist of Representatives of the Members of the League.

2. The Assembly shall meet at stated intervals and from time to time as occasion may require at the Seat of the League or at such other place as may be decided upon.

3. The Assembly may deal at its meetings with any matter within the sphere of action of the League or affecting the peace of the world.

4. At meetings of the Assembly, each Member of the League shall have one vote, and may have not more than three representatives.

ARTICLE IV

1. The Council shall consist of Representatives of the Principal Allied and Associated Powers,[1] together with Representatives of four other Members of the League. These four Members of the League shall be selected by the Assembly from time to time in its discretion. Until the appointment of the Representatives of the four Members of the League first selected by the Assembly, Representatives of Belgium, Brazil, Spain and Greece shall be members of the Council.

2. With the approval of the majority of the Assembly,

[1] The Principal Allied and Associated Powers are the following: The United States of America, the British Empire, France, Italy, and Japan (see Preamble of the Treaty of Peace with Germany).

the Council may name additional Members of the League whose Representatives shall always be Members of the Council;[1] the Council with like approval may increase the number of Members of the League to be selected by the Assembly for representation on the Council.[2]

2 *bis.*[3] *The Assembly shall fix by a two-thirds majority the rules dealing with the election of the non-permanent Members of the Council, and particularly such regulations as relate to their term of office and the conditions of re-eligibility.*

3. The Council shall meet from time to time as occasion may require, and at least once a year, at the Seat of the League, or at such other place as may be decided upon.

4. The Council may deal at its meetings with any matter within the sphere of action of the League or affecting the peace of the world.

5. Any Member of the League not represented on the Council shall be invited to send a Representative to sit as a member at any meeting of the Council during the consideration of matters specially affecting the interests of that Member of the League.

6. At meetings of the Council, each Member of the League represented on the Council shall have one vote, and may have not more than one Representative.

ARTICLE V

1. Except where otherwise expressly provided in this Covenant or by the terms of the present Treaty, decisions

[1] In virtue of this paragraph of the Covenant, Germany was nominated as a permanent Member of the Council on September 8, 1926.

[2] The number of Members of the Council selected by the Assembly was increased to six instead of four by virtue of a resolution adopted at the Third Ordinary Meeting of the Assembly on September 25, 1922. By a resolution taken by the Assembly on September 8, 1926, the number of Members of the Council selected by the Assembly was increased to nine.

[3] This Amendment came into force on July 29, 1926, in accordance with Article XXVI of the Covenant.

at any meeting of the Assembly or of the Council shall require the agreement of all the Members of the League represented at the meeting.

2. All matters of procedure at meetings of the Assembly or of the Council, including the appointment of Committees to investigate particular matters, shall be regulated by the Assembly or by the Council and may be decided by a majority of the Members of the League represented at the meeting.

3. The first meeting of the Assembly and the first meeting of the Council shall be summoned by the President of the United States of America.

ARTICLE VI

1. The permanent Secretariat shall be established at the Seat of the League. The Secretariat shall comprise a Secretary-General and such secretaries and staff as may be required.

2. The first Secretary-General shall be the person named in the Annex; thereafter the Secretary-General shall be appointed by the Council with the approval of the majority of the Assembly.

3. The secretaries and staff of the Secretariat shall be appointed by the Secretary-General with the approval of the Council.

4. The Secretary-General shall act in that capacity at all meetings of the Assembly and of the Council.

5.[1] *The expenses of the League shall be borne by the Members of the League in the proportion decided by the Assembly.*

[1] This Amendment came into force on August 13, 1924, in accordance with Article XXVI of the Covenant and replaces the following paragraph:—

"5. The expenses of the Secretariat shall be borne by the Members of the League in accordance with the apportionment of the expenses of the International Bureau of the Universal Postal Union."

ARTICLE VII

1. The Seat of the League is established at Geneva.

2. The Council may at any time decide that the Seat of the League shall be established elsewhere.

3. All positions under or in connection with the League, including the Secretariat, shall be open equally to men and women.

4. Representatives of the Members of the League and officials of the League when engaged on the business of the League shall enjoy diplomatic privileges and immunities.

5. The buildings and other property occupied by the League or its officials or by Representatives attending its meetings shall be inviolable.

ARTICLE VIII

1. The Members of the League recognize that the maintenance of peace requires the reduction of national armaments to the lowest point consistent with national safety and the enforcement by common action of international obligations.

2. The Council, taking account of the geographical situation and circumstances of each State, shall formulate plans for such reduction for the consideration and action of the several Governments.

3. Such plans shall be subject to reconsideration and revision at least every ten years.

4. After these plans shall have been adopted by the several Governments, the limits of armaments therein fixed shall not be exceeded without the concurrence of the Council.

5. The Members of the League agree that the manufacture by private enterprise of munitions and implements of war is open to grave objections. The Council shall advise how the evil effects attendant upon such manufacture can be prevented, due regard being had to the necessities of those Members of the League which are not able to manu-

facture the munitions and implements of war necessary for their safety.

6. The Members of the League undertake to interchange full and frank information as to the scale of their armaments, their military, naval, and air programmes and the condition of such of their industries as are adaptable to warlike purposes.

ARTICLE IX

A permanent Commission shall be constituted to advise the Council on the execution of the provisions of Articles I and VIII and on military, naval, and air questions generally.

ARTICLE X

The Members of the League undertake to respect and preserve as against external aggression the territorial integrity and existing political independence of all Members of the League. In case of any such aggression or in case of any threat or danger of such aggression the Council shall advise upon the means by which this obligation shall be fulfilled.

ARTICLE XI

1. Any war or threat of war, whether immediately affecting any of the Members of the League or not, is hereby declared a matter of concern to the whole League, and the League shall take any action that may be deemed wise and effectual to safeguard the peace of nations. In case any such emergency should arise the Secretary-General shall on the request of any Member of the League forthwith summon a meeting of the Council.

2. It is also declared to be the friendly right of each Member of the League to bring to the attention of the Assembly or of the Council any circumstance whatever affecting international relations which threatens to disturb international peace or the good understanding between nations upon which peace depends.

ARTICLE XII[1]

1. The Members of the League agree that if there should arise between them any dispute likely to lead to a rupture

---

[1] The Amendments printed in italics relating to these Articles came into force on September 26, 1924, in accordance with Article XXVI of the Covenant and replace the following texts:—

"ARTICLE XII

"The Members of the League agree that if there should arise between them any dispute likely to lead to a rupture they will submit the matter either to arbitration or to enquiry by the Council, and they agree in no case to resort to war until three months after the award by the arbitrators or the report by the Council.

"In any case under this Article the award of the arbitrators shall be made within a reasonable time, and the report of the Council shall be made within six months after the submission of the dispute."

"ARTICLE XIII

"The Members of the League agree that whenever any dispute shall arise between them which they recognize to be suitable for submission to arbitration and which cannot be satisfactorily settled by diplomacy, they will submit the whole subject-matter to arbitration.

"Disputes as to the interpretation of a treaty, as to any question of international law, as to the existence of any fact which if established would constitute a breach of any international obligation, or as to the extent and nature of the reparation to be made for any such breach, are declared to be among those which are generally suitable for submission to arbitration.

"For the consideration of any such dispute, the court of arbitration to which the case is referred shall be the court agreed on by the parties to the dispute or stipulated in any convention existing between them.

"The Members of the League agree that they will carry out in full good faith any award that may be rendered and that they will not resort to war against a Member of the League which complies therewith. In the event of any failure to carry out such an award, the Council shall propose what steps should be taken to give effect thereto."

they will submit the matter either to arbitration *or judicial settlement* or to enquiry by the Council, and they agree in no case to resort to war until three months after the award by the arbitrators *or the judicial decision* or the report by the Council.

2. In any case under this Article the award of the arbitrators *or the judicial decision* shall be made within a reasonable time, and the report of the Council shall be made within six months after the submission of the dispute.

ARTICLE XIII[1]

1. The Members of the League agree that whenever any dispute shall arise between them which they recognize to be suitable for submission to arbitration *or judicial settlement,* and which cannot be satisfactorily settled by diplomacy, they will submit the whole subject-matter to arbitration *or judicial settlement.*

2. Disputes as to the interpretation of a treaty, as to any question of international law, as to the existence of any fact which, if established would constitute a breach of any international obligation, or as to the extent and nature of the reparation to be made for any such breach, are declared to be among those which are generally suitable for submission to arbitration *or judicial settlement.*

3. *For the consideration of any such dispute, the court to which the case is referred shall be the Permanent Court of International Justice, established in accordance with Article XIV, or any tribunal agreed on by the parties to the dispute or stipulated in any convention existing between them.*

4. The Members of the League agree that they will carry out in full good faith any award *or decision* that may be rendered, and that they will not resort to war against a Member of the League which complies therewith. In the event of any failure to carry out such an award *or decision,* the Council shall propose what steps should be taken to give effect thereto.

[1] See note on page 285.

ARTICLE XIV

The Council shall formulate and submit to the Members of the League for adoption plans for the establishment of a Permanent Court of International Justice. The Court shall be competent to hear and determine any dispute of an international character which the parties thereto submit to it. The Court may also give an advisory opinion upon any dispute or question referred to it by the Council or by the Assembly.

ARTICLE XV

1.[1] If there should arise between Members of the League any dispute likely to lead to a rupture, which is not submitted to arbitration *or judicial settlement* in accordance with Article XIII, the Members of the League agree that they will submit the matter to the Council. Any party to the dispute may effect such submission by giving notice of the existence of the dispute to the Secretary-General, who will make all necessary arrangements for a full investigation and consideration thereof.

2. For this purpose the parties to the dispute will communicate to the Secretary-General, as promptly as possible, statements of their case with all the relevant facts and papers, and the Council may forthwith direct the publication thereof.

[1] The Amendment to the first paragraph of this Article came into force on September 26, 1924, in accordance with Article XXVI of the Covenant, and replaces the following text:—

"ARTICLE XV

"If there should arise between Members of the League any dispute likely to lead to a rupture, which is not submitted to arbitration in accordance with Article XIII, the Members of the League agree that they will submit the matter to the Council. Any party to the dispute may effect such submission by giving notice of the existence of the dispute to the Secretary-General, who will make all necessary arrangements for a full investigation and consideration thereof."

3. The Council shall endeavour to effect a settlement of the dispute, and if such efforts are successful, a statement shall be made public giving such facts and explanations regarding the dispute and the terms of settlement thereof as the Council may deem appropriate.

4. If the dispute is not thus settled, the Council either unanimously or by a majority vote shall make and publish a report containing a statement of the facts of the dispute and the recommendations which are deemed just and proper in regard thereto.

5. Any Member of the League represented on the Council may make public a statement of the facts of the dispute and of its conclusions regarding the same.

6. If a report by the Council is unanimously agreed to by the members thereof other than the Representatives of one or more of the parties to the dispute, the Members of the League agree that they will not go to war with any party to the dispute which complies with the recommendations of the report.

7. If the Council fails to reach a report which is unanimously agreed to by the members thereof, other than the Representatives of one or more of the parties to the dispute, the Members of the League reserve to themselves the right to take such action as they shall consider necessary for the maintenance of right and justice.

8. If the dispute between the parties is claimed by one of them, and is found by the Council, to arise out of a matter which by international law is solely within the domestic jurisdiction of that party, the Council shall so report, and shall make no recommendation as to its settlement.

9 The Council may in any case under this Article refer the dispute to the Assembly. The dispute shall be so referred at the request of either party to the dispute provided that such request be made within fourteen days after the submission of the dispute to the Council.

10. In any case referred to the Assembly, all the provisions of this Article and of Article XII relating to the action and powers of the Council shall apply to the action

and powers of the Assembly, provided that a report made by the Assembly, if concurred in by the Representatives of those Members of the League represented on the Council and of a majority of the other Members of the League, exclusive in each case of the Representatives of the parties to the dispute, shall have the same force as a report by the Council concurred in by all the members thereof other than the Representatives of one or more of the parties to the dispute.

ARTICLE XVI

1. Should any Member of the League resort to war in disregard of its covenants under Articles XII, XIII, or XV, it shall *ipso facto* be deemed to have committed an act of war against all other Members of the League, which hereby undertake immediately to subject it to the severance of all trade or financial relations, the prohibition of all intercourse between their nationals and the nationals of the covenant-breaking State, and the prevention of all financial, commercial, or personal intercourse between the nationals of the covenant-breaking State and the nationals of any other State, whether a Member of the League or not.

2 It shall be the duty of the Council in such case to recommend to the several Governments concerned what effective military, naval, or air force the Members of the League shall severally contribute to the armed forces to be used to protect the covenants of the League.

3. The Members of the League agree, further, that they will mutually support one another in the financial and economic measures which are taken under this article, in order to minimize the loss and inconvenience resulting from the above measures, and that they will mutually support one another in resisting any special measures aimed at one of their number by the covenant-breaking State, and that they will take the necessary steps to afford passage through their territory to the forces of any of the

Members of the League which are co-operating to protect the covenants of the League.

4. Any Member of the League which has violated any covenant of the League may be declared to be no longer a Member of the League by a vote of the Council concurred in by the Representatives of all the other Members of the League represented thereon.

ARTICLE XVII

1. In the event of a dispute between a Member of the League and a State which is not a Member of the League, or between States not Members of the League, the State or States not Members of the League shall be invited to accept the obligations of membership in the League for the purposes of such dispute, upon such conditions as the Council may deem just. If such invitation is accepted the provisions of Articles XII to XVI inclusive shall be applied with such modifications as may be deemed necessary by the Council.

2. Upon such invitation being given the Council shall immediately institute an enquiry into the circumstances of the dispute and recommend such action as may seem best and most effectual in the circumstances.

3. If a State so invited shall refuse to accept the obligations of membership in the League for the purposes of such dispute, and shall resort to war against a Member of the League, the provisions of Article XVI shall be applicable as against the State taking such action.

4. If both parties to the dispute when so invited refuse to accept the obligations of membership in the League for the purposes of such dispute, the Council may take such measures and make such recommendations as will prevent hostilities and will result in the settlement of the dispute.

ARTICLE XVIII

Every treaty or international engagement entered into hereafter by any Member of the League shall be forthwith registered with the Secretariat and shall as soon as possible be published by it. No such treaty or international engagement shall be binding until so registered.

ARTICLE XIX

The Assembly may from time to time advise the reconsideration by Members of the League of treaties which have become inapplicable and the consideration of international conditions whose continuance might endanger the peace of the world.

ARTICLE XX

1. The Members of the League severally agree that this Covenant is accepted as abrogating all obligations or understandings *inter se* which are inconsistent with the terms thereof, and solemnly undertake that they will not hereafter enter into any engagements inconsistent with the terms thereof.

2. In case any Member of the League shall, before becoming a Member of the League, have undertaken any obligations inconsistent with the terms of this Covenant, it shall be the duty of such Member to take immediate steps to procure its release from such obligations.

ARTICLE XXI

Nothing in this Covenant shall be deemed to affect the validity of international engagements, such as treaties of arbitration or regional understandings like the Monroe doctrine, for securing the maintenance of peace.

ARTICLE XXII

1. To those colonies and territories which as a consequence of the late war have ceased to be under the sovereignty of the States which formerly governed them and which are inhabited by peoples not yet able to stand by them-

selves under the strenuous conditions of the modern world, there should be applied the principle that the well-being and development of such peoples form a sacred trust of civilization and that securities for the performance of this trust should be embodied in this Covenant.

2. The best method of giving practical effect to this principle is that the tutelage of such peoples should be entrusted to advanced nations who by reason of their resources, their experience, or their geographical position can best undertake this responsibility, and who are willing to accept it, and that this tutelage should be exercised by them as Mandatories on behalf of the League.

3. The character of the mandate must differ according to the stage of the development of the people, the geographical situation of the territory, its economic conditions, and other similar circumstances.

4. Certain communities formerly belonging to the Turkish Empire have reached a stage of development where their existence as independent nations can be provisionally recognized subject to the rendering of administrative advice and assistance by a Mandatory until such time as they are able to stand alone. The wishes of these communities must be a principal consideration in the selection of the Mandatory.

5. Other peoples, especially those of Central Africa, are at such a stage that the Mandatory must be responsible for the administration of the territory under conditions which will guarantee freedom of conscience and religion, subject only to the maintenance of public order and morals, the prohibition of abuses such as the slave trade, the arms traffic and the liquor traffic, and the prevention of the establishment of fortifications or military and naval bases, and of military training of the natives for other than police purposes and the defence of territory, and will also secure equal opportunities for the trade and commerce of other Members of the League.

6. There are territories, such as South-West Africa and certain of the South Pacific Islands, which, owing to the

sparseness of their population, or their small size, or their remoteness from the centres of civilization, or their geographical contiguity to the territory of the Mandatory, and other circumstances, can be best administered under the laws of the Mandatory as integral portions of its territory, subject to the safeguards above mentioned in the interests of the indigenous population.

7. In every case of mandate the Mandatory shall render to the Council an annual report in reference to the territory committed to its charge.

8. The degree of authority, control, or administration to be exercised by the Mandatory shall, if not previously agreed upon by the Members of the League, be explicitly defined in each case by the Council.

9. A permanent Commission shall be constituted to receive and examine the annual reports of the Mandatories and to advise the Council on all matters relating to the observance of the mandates.

ARTICLE XXIII

Subject to and in accordance with the provisions of international conventions existing or hereafter to be agreed upon, the Members of the League:

(a) will endeavour to secure and maintain fair and humane conditions of labour for men, women, and children, both in their own countries and in all countries to which their commercial and industrial relations extend, and for that purpose will establish and maintain the necessary international organizations;

(b) undertake to secure just treatment of the native inhabitants of territories under their control;

(c) will entrust the League with the general supervision over the execution of agreements with regard to the traffic in women and children, and the traffic in opium and other dangerous drugs;

(d) will entrust the League with the general supervision of the trade in arms and ammunition with the countries in which the control of this traffic is necessary in the common interest;

(e) will make provision to secure and maintain freedom of communications and of transit and equitable treatment for the commerce of all Members of the League. In this connection, the special necessities of the regions devastated during the war of 1914–1918 shall be borne in mind;

(f) will endeavour to take steps in matters of international concern for the prevention and control of disease.

ARTICLE XXIV

1. There shall be placed under the direction of the League all international bureaux already established by general treaties if the parties to such treaties consent. All such international bureaux and all commissions for the regulation of matters of international interest hereafter constituted shall be placed under the direction of the League.

2. In all matters of international interest which are regulated by general conventions but which are not placed under the control of international bureaux or commissions, the Secretariat of the League shall, subject to the consent of the Council and if desired by the parties, collect and distribute all relevant information and shall render any other assistance which may be necessary or desirable.

3. The Council may include as part of the expenses of the Secretariat the expenses of any bureau or commission which is placed under the direction of the League.

ARTICLE XXV

The Members of the League agree to encourage and promote the establishment and co-operation of duly authorized voluntary national Red Cross organizations having as purposes the improvement of health, the prevention of disease, and the mitigation of suffering throughout the world.

ARTICLE XXVI

1. Amendments to this Covenant will take effect when ratified by the Members of the League whose Representatives compose the Council and by a majority of the Members of the League whose Representatives compose the Assembly.

2. No such amendments shall bind any Member of the League which signifies its dissent therefrom, but in that case it shall cease to be a Member of the League.

INDEX

Aaland Islands dispute, the, 187
aggression, test of, 214–17
alliances, military, 273–4
Allied and Associated Powers, the, 280 n.
Allied Maritime Transport Council, the, 19–20, 22, 27, 165
amendments to Article XVI, 207 n., 209 n
America, 28–9, 45 et seq., 54, 61, 87, 88–90, 92, 102, 103, 108, 183–4, 189 et seq., 208, 211, 220, 230 et seq., 248, 261, 266, 269, 274–7, 282
  and League sanctions, 58, 143, 158
  representation of, at League world conferences, 57 n.
American capital in Europe, investment of, 90
Anglo-American Treaty of Guarantee to France, 158
Anglo-French naval compromise of 1928, 238
Approach to World Unity, Sweetser's, 203
arbitration, 48 et seq., 204, 209, 217–18, 221, 225, 285–6
Arbitration and Security Committee (1928), 218 n., 222 n., 223 n., 225
Argentina, 53, 59 n., 63
armaments, growth of, 273
Arnold-Forster, W., 270 n.
Article V, 191, 281–2
Article VIII, 198, 283–4

Article X, 142, 170, 177–8, 185, 195, 196 n., 197 n., 206, 284
Article XI, 143, 170, 174, 179–81, 186–8, 206, 209–11, 213, 214, 249, 284
Article XII, 145, 192, 194, 285
Article XIII, 143, 145, 192, 285 n., 286
Article XV, 143, 178, 193, 197, 208, 287–9
Article XVI, 142, 143 et seq., 158 et seq., 172, 173, 175, 194, 204, 206 et seq., 258, 259, 269, 274, 277, 289–90
Article XVII, 146, 194, 197, 290
Article XIX, 196, 291
Article XXIII, 39
Article XXXIII, 265 n.
Article XXXIV, 265 n.
Assembly of the League, the, 17 n., 27, 44, 82, 129, 280
Austria, 33, 37, 95

"balance of power," 219 n.
Balfour, Lord, 125
Belgian Relief Commission, 252, 259, 265 n.
Belgium, 234–5, 243
Bilateral action re tariffs, 85, 87
blockade, 58–9, 144, 154–7, 165, 183–4, 191, 201, 214, 258, 259, 264, 266–9
Blockade Commission, 157, 158
Blockade Committee, Executive, 156–7, 165
Blockade Council, 165, 183
Blockade Intelligence Committee, 154–5

Bolivia, 61 *n.*
Borah, Senator, 228, 232, 262
Brazil, 53, 54 *n* , 59 *n*
Briand, M., 83, 96, 105, 123, 124, 221 *n.*, 228, 229
Briand Memorandum (May 1930), 105 *et seq.*
"British Monroe Doctrine," the, 238, 240, 249, 250
Brussels Conference, the, 43
Bulgaria, 170

Capper, Senator, 262
Cecil, Viscount, 270 *n.*
Chamberlain, Sir Austen, 13, 71, 72 *n.*, 82, 215 *n* , 242, 249
China, 53, 54 *n.*, 63, 73 *n.*, 74, 248, 249
"collective" system, strengthening of the, 274
colonies and Dominions, 102
Comert, M. Pierre, 76
Commission Internationale de Ravitaillement, the, 19
communications, control of, 153 *n.*
confidence, want of, among European countries, 273–5
Consultative Trade Organizations, 29
"contact," international, 77–80
contraband, 264
Convention of Financial Assistance, 212 *n.*
Coolidge Naval Conference, the, 204
Coolidge, President, 45, 54, 58
Coudenhove - Kalergi, Count, 83
Council Committee System, the, 66 *et seq.*

Council meetings, question of number, 72 *et seq.*, 82
Council of the League, Executive, 17 *n.*, 27, 110, 128, 156 *n.*, 280–1
Covenant of the League, 141–3, 196, 200–1, 236, 239, 243, 247, 260, 267, 279–95
Covenant, the gap in the, 245, 246, 268
Covenant, proposed amendment of the, 250–1, 263
Customs Formalities Convention, 33, 36, 39
Czechoslovakia, 89

Danzig, 66
Declaration of London (1909), 264, 265, 266
denationalization of the League staff, dangers of, 17
Disarmament, 64, 65, 204–5, 273
Disarmament Conference, the, 57, 64, 204, 248
Drummond, Sir Eric, 137

economic boycott, 48–50
Economic Conference, General, 32, 35, 36, 38, 40–4
Economic Consultative Committee (May 1929), 85, 97
economic co-operation, 108
economic reconstruction a task for individuals, 34, 37
economic weapons of the League, 142 *et seq.*
  blockade, 144, 148, 149, 151, 154–7
  severance of financial relations, 150

economic weapons of the League—*continued*
Export and Import prohibition, 150, 165
"rationing" system, 150–1
search by Naval Forces, 153
cable and mail censorship, 153
food-supplies, cutting off of, 252

economic work of a League, 24, 33, 37, 39–40

Egypt, 249

Entente Cordiale, the, 219 *n.*

Europe and the economic problem, 108–10

Europe, rival armed camps of, 219–20

European Commission, establishment of a, 124

European Federal Union, 83, 105

European organization of the League, external, 110 *et seq.*

evacuation of the Rhineland, 105

exchanges, European, 36, 37, 47

Financial Reconstruction, 36, 74

financial systems a matter for Governments, 33

food ships, immunity of, 252 *et seq.*

food-supplies, differentiation between civilian and military destination, 253, 257, 259, 265 *n.*

Foreign Ministers and Council attendances, 73–4, 79–80, 108

France, 89, 105, 111, 158, 218, 221, 233, 234–5, 244, 274

Franco-German frontier, the, 222, 226

"Freedom of the Seas," 262 *et seq.*

French Disarmament Plan (1932), the, 216 *n.*

French Memorandum of May 1930, the, 105 *et seq*

gas in war, use of, 256

Geneva—
National Secretaries at, 13, 25–6
as Headquarters of the League, 13, 18, 29, 65, 77, 79

Geneva Protocol, the, 159 *et seq.*, 204

Genoa, Conference of, 35

Germany, 54 *n.*, 55, 63, 69, 89, 137, 169, 242, 265, 266 *n.*, 274, 281 *n.*

Gibson, Mr., 276

Great Britain, 120–1, 123, 142–3, 181, 183, 204–5, 208, 211, 240, 249, 261, 263, 264, 266–8, 274–5

Great War, causes of the, 219, 220

Greco-Bulgar incident, the, 170 *et seq.*, 215, 242

Grey, Sir E., 219 *n.*, 265 *n.*

Hankow, 74 *n.*

Henderson, Mr., 82, 263

Herriot, M., 83

Holland, 123

Hoover Moratorium (1931), 275 *n.*

Hoover, President, 252, 254, 258, 260–1
"humanization" of war, 255
Hungary, 33, 37, 66, 68, 69

Immigration, 56, 62
Imports and Exports Prohibitions Convention, the, 94
International Administration in the War, Allied, 19–22
International Blockade Committee of 1921, 167
international character of the League Secretariat, 125, 128, 130, 137
international conception of the League, 15, 23, 27, 47
International Labour Office, 125, 138
Italy, 102, 123, 137, 158, 218

Japan, 187, 197 n., 249, 250

Kellogg Pact, the, 205, 215 n., 228 et seq., 257, 259, 260, 263, 266, 269, 271, 275–7

Labour Party, British, 263
Lansdowne, Lord, 219 n.
Latin America, 59 et seq.
League Model Treaties, 218, 226 n.
League of Nations, the—
  danger of its becoming a political backwater, 13, 18
  its relation to National Governments, 14, 16, 17, 25, 27–8, 129, 148
  as a factor in international policies, 14–16, 22, 27, 47, 79, 80

League of Nations, the—contd.
  handicapped by its location, 13, 16, 29
  Assembly of, 17, 27, 82, 118, 129
  Council of, 17 n., 27, 65 et seq., 82, 110, 118, 128, 156 n.
  as an improved Hague Tribunal, 16, 18
  its economic work, 23–4, 30, 33, 39–40, 44, 95 et seq., 108 et seq.
  its dependence on public opinion, 24–5, 27, 40, 272
  its relation to the Press, 27
  and America, 28–9, 45 et seq., 54 et seq., 143, 189 et seq., 231 et seq., 249, 271
  Research Division in, importance of a, 30
  and the preservation of peace, 47, 53, 114, 141, 170, 185, 188, 220, 284
  and a universal world pledge, 51–2
  its framework should be universal, 54, 65
  admission of Germany to, 54 n., 55, 63
  and blockade decisions, 58
  and Latin America, 59 et seq.
  and China, 63–4
  and Soviet Russia, 64–5
  the author's conception of its international rôle, 76–7
  and the tariffs question, 95 et seq.
  and France, 111
  European external organization of, 110–13, 117, 118, 120

League of Nations, the—*contd.*
  and "regional" questions, 115, 120, 222–3
  and "universal" questions, 116, 201, 221, 222, 273
  and Great Britain, 120–1
  Secretariat of, 124, 125 *et seq.*
  sanction of, 141, 142, 146, 158–9, 160–1, 164, 167 *n.*, 169, 173, 175, 176, 205, 211, 236–7, 268
  economic weapons of, 142 *et seq*, 163–7, 176, 210, 253
  obligations of membership of, 147, 199, 206, 211, 246
  the Geneva Protocol, 162 *et seq.*
  Intelligence Department of, 166, 168
  and the Greco-Bulgar incident, 170 *et seq.*
  Article X, ambiguity of, 177, 185, 197 *n.*
  fundamental principle of, 190
  unanimity in decisions of, 191, 201, 282
  financial assistance of, 212 *n.*, 213, 214
  and the Kellogg Pact, 231 *et seq.*
League of Nations Societies, 26
legal effects of League action, consideration of, 163, 166, 173, 183, 185
legal provisions of the League, analysis of the, 190–6
"Letters of Assurance," 151 *n.*
Lloyd George, Mr., 221 *n.*
Locarno Agreement, the, 169, 185, 222, 226
Lytton Commission, the, 186

MacDonald, Mr. Ramsay, 248, 263
Manchuria, 248, 250
mandatory colonies, 23, 291–3
Matsuoka, M., 250
Membership of the League, 279
monopolies, 99
Monroe Doctrine, the, 53, 60, 241, 245, 277
Most-Favoured Nation Clause, 85, 87–8, 92–5, 99, 101
Multilateral action *re* tariffs, 85–7, 94
munitions, 198, 272, 283
Mutual Assistance, Treaty of, 159

Nansen, Dr. 217 *n.*
national disputes, localized, 47–8
National Secretaries, Geneva, 13, 25
National Secretaries, Home, 26–7
naval blockade, 166
naval demonstrations, 172, 174, 176, 177, 179, 180, 188
Naval Disarmament Conference, the, 254, 262
naval problem, the, 269–70
"no discrimination," tariff, 87–8
Norway, 136, 142

Pacific Agreement, the, 261
Panama Treaty of July, 1926, 60 *n.*
Pangalos, General, 170–1
percentage reductions, tariff, 100–1
Permanent Court of International Justice, the, 261, 286, 287

Peru, 249
Phillimore, Lord, 143
pledge, universal world, 50–2
Poland, 54 *n.*, 206
political co-operation, European, 107
Press, the, 27
private interests and tariffs, 86, 108
public opinion and the League, 24–5, 27, 40

"reciprocity," tariff, 87–8
Recovery: The Second Effort, Sir A. Salter's, 271
Red Cross, the, 256, 294
"regional" and "universal" problem of the League, the, 116, 120
"regional" League, dangers of a, 53
Reparations, 105
reserves of the Kellogg Pact, 236 *et seq.*
"Rights and Obligations," 243-5
Roosevelt, President, 142
Russia, Soviet, 57 *n*, 64–5, 123, 220
Rutgers Memorandum of 1928, the, 206, 212 *n.*

St. Germain, Treaty of, 95
Sanctions Clauses of the Covenant, 142, 146, 159, 160–1, 175 *n.*
Secretariat, the League, 282
and the European Commission, 124
its international character, 125, 128, 130
recruitment to the staff of, 126

Secretariat, the League—*contd.*
resident representation, 132–4
organization of, 137
"declaration of loyalty," officials', 138
security, collective, 158–9, 204–5
self-defence, right of, 215 *n.*, 241
separatism developed by the War, 15
"shadow councils" of the League, 133–4
Sino-Japanese conflict, the, 185, 186, 196 *n.*, 248, 271
Smith, Mr. Jeremiah, 37
South American States, 53, 54
Spain, 54 *n.*, 89, 137
Special meetings of the Council, 75–6
Stimson, Mr., 59 *n.*, 205, 248, 271
Stresemann, Dr., 83
Supreme Economic Council, the, 22, 27, 31
Sweden, 217 *n.*
Switzerland, 64, 65

Taft, President, 142
tariff, the American, 88–9, 93, 102–3
tariffs, 35, 38, 44, 84 *et seq.*, 91–4, 99–102, 108–9
Trade barriers, *see under Tariffs*
"Triple Pact" of 1919, the, 221
Turkey, 123, 292

Under-Secretary-General, post of, 137
unilateral action *re* tariffs, 84, 87
"unilateral" engagements, 224, 226
United States, *see under America*

"United States of Europe," 90–2

"universal" Protocol of 1924, the, 221

war—
  conditional right of, 208 *n*.
  criminality of, 255
  outlawry of, 235, 239, 256
  prevention of, 53, 114, 141, 143, 172, 179, 185, 187, 188, 199, 203, 205, 215, 216, 220, 248

Wilhelmina case, the, 265 *n*.
Wilson, President, 24, 142, 196 *n*., 248, 262
World Economic Conference of May 1927, 56, 84, 97, 98
world opinion, Economic Conference to be a forum of, 40–1, 43
world peace, 50–2

Young Plan, the, 105

Zollvereins, 91–2, 95

GEORGE ALLEN & UNWIN LTD
LONDON 40 MUSEUM STREET, W C.1
CAPE TOWN. 73 ST. GEORGE'S STREET
SYDNEY, N S.W: WYNYARD SQUARE
AUCKLAND, N.Z.. 41 ALBERT STREET
TORONTO. 91 WELLINGTON STREET, WEST